BRAIN GAMES!

Ready-to-Use
Activities That Make Thinking <u>Fun</u>
for Grades 6-12

JACK UMSTATTER

JOSSEY-BASS
A Wiley Imprint
www.josseybass.com

Published by Jossey-Bass
A Wiley Imprint
989 Market Street, San Francisco, CA 94103-1741   www.josseybass.com

Jossey-Bass books and products are available through most bookstores. To contact Jossey-Bass directly call our Customer Care Department within the U.S. at (800) 956-7739, outside the U.S. at (317) 572-3986 or fax (317) 572-4002.

Jossey-Bass also publishes its books in a variety of electronic formats. Some content that appears in print may not be available in electronic books.

Library of Congress Cataloging-in-Publication Data

Umstatter, Jack.
    Brain games! : ready-to-use activities that make thinking fun, grades 6–12 /
    by Jack Umstatter.
        p.   cm.
    ISBN 0-87628-187-0 (spiral wire).—ISBN 0-87628-125-0 (pbk.)
    1. Educational games.   2. Creative activities and seat work.   3. Word games
    4. Thought and thinking—Study and teaching (Elementary)   I. Title.
    LB1029.G3U67   1996   95-49674
    371.3'97—dc20

Printed in the United States of America
FIRST EDITION
PB Printing 10 9 8 7 6 5

DEDICATION

Thanks to Chris, Kate, and Maureen for their help and support in this effort.

ACKNOWLEDGMENTS

Thanks again to Win Huppuch and Connie Kallback for their insight and guidance.

To Celeste Perri for her poem, "Agamemnon," used in Activity #5 in this resource.

To Doug Breckner for his assistance with Section Five, "Math."

To all the teachers who continue to inspire their students to think critically and have fun at the same time.

To my students who have made teaching an enjoyable and memorable experience.

Special thanks to Dover Publications for the use of illustrations from the Dover Clip Art Series.

The questions in exercise 51, "Scientific Things to Think About," are used with permission from *Science Is: A Source Book of Fascinating Facts, Projects and Activities*, by Susan V. Bosak, 515 pages. Copyright 1992, New York, NY: Scholastic, 1-800-325-6149.

ABOUT THE AUTHOR

Jack Umstatter has taught English and literature on both the junior and senior high school levels since 1972 and education at Dowling College in Oakdale, New York, for the past seven years. He is currently teaching in the Cold Spring Harbor School District in New York.

Mr. Umstatter graduated from Manhattan College with a B.A. in English and completed his M.A. in English at S.U.N.Y-Stony Brook. He earned his Educational Administration degree at Long Island University.

A member of Phi Delta Kappa and the National Council of Teachers of English, Mr. Umstatter has been elected to *Who's Who Among America's Teachers*. He has taught all levels of secondary English classes, including the Honors and Advanced Placement Literature classes. As coach of the high school's academic team, the Brainstormers, he led the team in capturing the Long Island and New York State championships when competing in the American Scholastic Competition Network National Tournament of Champions in Lake Forest, Illinois.

Mr. Umstatter is the author of *Hooked on Literature!* and *201 Ready-to-Use Word Games for the English Classroom*, both C.A.R.E. publications.

ABOUT THIS RESOURCE

"If you can fill the unforgiving minute
With sixty seconds' worth of distance run . . ."

These lines from Rudyard Kipling's memorable poem, "If," send a message to all of us who teach. Time is valuable, time is precious, time is to be used well. *That* time can be classroom time, lesson preparation time, or, just as importantly, your personal time, something we seem to have in such small amounts these days.

Though we are constantly looking for classroom materials and lessons that will interest and challenge our students, the commitments of our daily lives do not always allow us to motivate, remediate, and captivate our students. We want our kids to be good thinkers and to perform to the best of their abilities.

Brain Games!, with 172 ready-to-use reproducible classroom activities, is designed to fill your extra classroom minutes with creative, challenging, and practical activities that will save you the unenviable task of having to prepare additional lessons. All that work has already been done for you! These fun activities, which have received very positive student response, are enjoyable exercises that will stimulate your students to think and reason more intelligently and critically. Time well spent . . . Kipling would have loved it!

These activities will increase your students' interest and knowledge in areas across the curriculum. Organized into seven sections that cover a wide variety of topics, *Brain Games!* will inform and challenge your students as they gain greater thinking skills and knowledge of the world around them. The section titles are "Listening and Remembering," "Across the Curriculum," "Language and Writing," "Logic and Reasoning," "Math," "The World Around You," and "Me." Many of the exercises involve real-life situations. Others deal with theoretical or hypothetical situations. All involve fun, a valuable component of productive classroom activities.

The first two sections contain a number of listening exercises to help students sharpen their listening skills and enjoy some challenge and fun at the same time. These sections begin with TEACHER DIRECTIONS that include questions and answers to go along with the reading sections.

You can choose the activity's implementation. Use it as a total group activity, a small group activity, or as an independent activity. Introduce a unit with it or use the exercise as a reinforcement or remediation. Why not distribute it as a homework assignment, enrichment, or extra credit? These activities help to prepare students for the types of thinking and reasoning skills necessary for maximum performance on standardized exams including state examinations, the SAT, and the ACT. They also make for effective substitute lesson plans, research work, or skill enhancers. Classroom competitions are not out of the question! The possibilities are numerous. Though some activities are best done with you as the facilitator, many can be done independently by the students. Answer Keys are located at the back of the book, except for answers to the listening exercises in the first two sections.

Brain Games! will prove to be beneficial for both you and your students. Not only will you have these ready-to-use, stimulating activities at your fingertips, but your students will also increase their knowledge and critical thinking skills. So go ahead and reap the benefits of *Brain Games!* It is time well spent.

Jack Umstatter

CONTENTS

SECTION ONE: LISTENING AND REMEMBERING 1

The Teacher Directions for the Section One Activities are as follows: The Teacher Directions for Activity 3 are found on page 3; for Activity 4 on page 3; for Activity 5 on page 4; for Activity 6 on page 4; for Activity 7 on page 5; for Activity 8 on page 7; for Activity 9 on page 8; for Activity 10 on page 9; for Activity 11 on page 9; for Activity 12 on page 10; for Activity 15 on page 11; for Activity 17 on page 12; for Activity 18 on page 12.

SECTION TWO: ACROSS THE CURRICULUM 33

The Teacher Directions for the Section Two Activities are as follows: The Teacher Directions for Activity 25 are found on page 35; for Activity 31 on page 36; for Activity 42 on page 37; for Activity 43 on page 39; for Activity 46 on page 40.

SECTION THREE: LANGUAGE AND WRITING 77

SECTION FOUR: LOGIC AND REASONING 115

SECTION FIVE: MATH 137

SECTION SIX: THE WORLD AROUND YOU 163

Contents

SECTION SEVEN: ME 197

ANSWER KEY 219

LISTENING AND REMEMBERING

TEACHER DIRECTIONS TO SECTION ONE: LISTENING AND REMEMBERING

Activity 3. Aesop's "The Two Travelers and the Bear"

Read Aesop's fable (activity 3 in this section) to the students. Then ask them the following questions, which can be answered orally or on a separate piece of paper. The correct answers follow the questions.

TEACHER'S QUESTIONS

1. Did the friends expect to see the bear? (no . . . "much to their surprise")
2. What two words describe the tree that the friend climbed? (big, stout)
3. Why did the one friend pretend to be dead? (". . . the bear would overtake him before he could hide . . .")
4. Was the friend who was lying on the ground original in his thought to pretend to be dead? (no . . . "because it is said that a bear will not touch a dead body.")
5. According to the story, where did the bear poke the man? (up and down)
6. Is the gender of the bear given? (no)
7. Describe the manner in which the bear left the man? (the bear "ambled" or moved slowly)
8. Where was the bear headed after its time with the man? (woods)
9. When did the man who had fled up the tree rejoin his friend? (after the bear left)
10. Which man was dusting himself off? (the one who pretended to be dead)

Activity 4. "Casey at the Bat"

Read the poem "Casey at the Bat" (activity 4 in this section) to the students. Then ask them the following questions, which can be answered orally or on a separate piece of paper. The correct answers follow the questions.

TEACHER'S QUESTIONS

1. To whom is the poet referring in the term, the "patrons of the game"? (spectators)
2. What "springs eternal in the human breast"? (hope)
3. How did Flynn and Blake surprise the crowd? (each reached base with hits)
4. Approximately how many were in attendance that day? (5,000)
5. With what mood did Casey approach the plate? (confidence since there was "ease in his manner," "pride in his bearing," and "a smile on Casey's face.")
6. When Casey heard the cheers as he came to bat, what did he do to his hat? ("doffed" it . . . took it off)

7. What is Casey's mood as he enters the batter's box? (Defiance is in his eye and a sneer curls his lip.)

8. What two terms does the poet use in place of the word "ball"? (leather-covered sphere, spheroid)

9. What was like the "beating of the storm waves on a stern and distant shore"? (the crowd's "muffled roar")

10. What are "clenched in hate"? (Casey's teeth)

Activity 5. "Agamemnon"

Read the poem "Agamemnon" (activity 5 in this section) to the students. Then ask them the following questions, which can be answered orally or on a separate piece of paper. The correct answers follow the questions.

TEACHER'S QUESTIONS

1. What is the mistake the poet thinks she might have made in naming the cat Agamemnon? (though the cat was named after a warrior, Agamemnon, the poet questions the naming.)

2. What are two activities Agamemnon enjoyed? (preying, pouncing, killing birds, making flesh welt, making grown men wince)

3. How does the poet show how small Agamemnon once was? (". . . could hide between Kafka and Virgil on my bookshelf or lose yourself in the folds of my pillows . . ."

4. How did Agamemnon comfort the poet? (Agamemnon would come and lie on the poet's chest when she was reading something awful. They would breathe together.)

5. What two words, both beginning with the letter *d*, does the poet use to contrast her feelings regarding Agamemnon and mice? (dear, dreadful)

6. Why did the poet give Agamemnon Meow Mix and a bowl of milk? (as a reward for killing a mouse)

7. Who accompanied the poet to the vet? (her mother)

8. How does the poet compare herself with Clytemnestra? (each had something to do with a killing, one deserved, the other undeserved.)

9. The poet refers to another cat's death. Thinking the cat that was killed on the road could have been Agamemnon, she arrives home to find her own cat doing what? (lazily lying on the couch)

10. What is the last image this poem conveys? (the poet goes home to a house that "is screaming your [Agamemnon's] absence.")

Activity 6. "Accidents Happen!"

Read the following accident account to the students. The students will then answer the twenty questions found on their activity 6 "Accidents Happen!" page in this section. The correct answers are found in the answer key.

TEACHER'S READING: "ACCIDENTS HAPPEN!"

Last Saturday, May 16, an accident involving three automobiles and four people occurred at the intersection of Washington Avenue and Clark Boulevard in Fultoness. The day was clear and sunny, and police authorities claim that the bright sun may have contributed to the accident.

Forty-five-year-old Steve Manning, owner of the popular restaurant, The Manor, was driving his car, a Hall Lion, in a southerly direction along Washington Avenue around five that afternoon. Driving in the opposite direction along Washington Avenue was Ms. Marcia Masterson, a twenty-year-old bank teller. According to Fultoness Police Chief Percy Tyler, Ms. Masterson was traveling with a male companion, Lyle Jackson, a painter, also twenty. Her car, a blue Gregson, was moving at the rate of thirty-five miles per hour when Ms. Masterson spotted a green Cemmo traveling westbound on Clark Boulevard one-hundred yards up on the right. Yves Neilson, the driver of this third car, claims that he was temporarily blinded by the bright sun and could not see that the traffic light at the corner of Clark and Washington was red. Assuming he had the right of way, Neilson drove his car into the intersection where his automobile struck the back door of the passenger side of Ms. Masterson's vehicle, forcing her car to then collide with the car driven by Mr. Manning, who had reached the intersection at the exact same time as the other two automobiles.

Mr. Manning suffered several abrasions on his arm, needed no further medical treatment, and was driven home from the accident by the police. Ms. Masterson and Mr. Jackson were both hurt in the accident. The former was hospitalized with a broken leg and the latter needed stitches in the right arm. Neilson was taken from the accident scene by ambulance and is reportedly in critical condition in nearby Mercy Hospital. Authorities announced that reports of the extent of his injuries will be released later tonight.

All three cars have been impounded by the police. Investigation of the accident will continue tomorrow. At this time none of the drivers has been charged.

Activity 7. Does It Look the Same?

Read the following eight directions to the students. The students will draw their figure in the space allotted on the activity 7 "Does It Look the Same?" page in this section. The accompanying figure is what the completed figure looks like.

TEACHER'S DIRECTIONS

1. In the middle of the page draw a square having sides of one inch.

2. Just above and a bit to the left of the upper left-hand corner of the square, print the letter A in its uppercase form. The letter should be about $\frac{1}{8}$ of an inch in height and half that distance away from the square. The letter should not touch the square.

3. Just above and a bit to the right of the right-hand corner of the square, print the letter B in its uppercase form. The letter should be about $\frac{1}{8}$ of an inch in height and half that distance away from the square. The letter should not touch the square.

4. Just to the right of the bottom right-hand corner of the square, print the letter C in its uppercase form. The letter should be about $\frac{1}{8}$ of an inch in height and should not touch the square. If the bottom line of the square were extended, it would bisect the letter C.

5. Just to the left of the bottom left-hand corner of the square, print the letter *D* in its uppercase form. The letter should be about ⅛ of an inch in height and should be half that distance away from the square's corner. If the bottom line of the square were to be continued, the line would bisect through the letter *D*. The letter should not touch the square.

6. From the midpoint of the top side of the square, draw a one-inch line that extends toward the top of the page.

7. Draw a circle the size of a penny so that it looks as if the circle is resting atop the line that you have just finished constructing.

8. Within this circle print the word "Hello" within the upper semicircle. The *H* is printed in its uppercase form and the remaining letters are printed in lowercase.

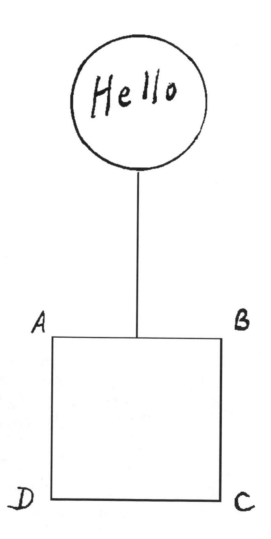

Activity 8. Listen and Make the Changes

Read the directions for each of the four sentences (one at a time) to the students. The correct answer for each sentence is given to you after the directions. The students will record their answers on the activity 8 "Listen and Make the Changes" page in this section.

TEACHER'S DIRECTIONS

For sentence 1:

1. Change the letter *b* to the letter *g*.
2. Drop the *i* and insert *wa* in its place.
3. Add the letter *e* in front of the letter *v*.
4. Add the word *in* as the fourth word of the sentence.
5. Add the letters *ir* to the end of the sentence's first word.
6. Drop the second letter of the sentence's last word and replace it with the letter combination *ed*.

The new sentence is: *Their goat was in every hedge.*

For sentence 2:

1. Drop the sentence's initial letter.
2. Drop the second word's first letter and add *ed* to the end of that word.
3. Retain only the third, ninth, tenth, and eleventh letters of the sentence's third word.
4. Insert the word *the* in front of the word you reconstructed in number three above.
5. Change the second letter of the original sentence's fourth word to the letter *n*.
6. Reverse the letter order of the original sentence's last word. Add the letter *w* after the letter *o* and then drop the word's first two letters.

The new sentence is: *He lowered the rent in town.*

For sentence 3:

1. Move the last two words to the front of the sentence.
2. Insert the word *and* between these two words.
3. Make the original sentence's first letter a lowercase letter.
4. In that same word drop the letter *e* and replace it with *ow*.
5. Make the *w* in "will" an uppercase letter.
6. Delete the letter *k* in the original sentence's third word and replace it with the letter combination *thes*.
7. Delete the word *the*.

The new sentence is: *Track and record how Will breathes.*

For sentence 4:

1. Delete the first three letters of the first word and replace them with the letters *lea*, with the *L* as an uppercase letter.
2. Replace the *gr* combination with an uppercase *N*.
3. Break the fourth word in half.
4. In the second of the two newly created words, insert the letter *w* between the *t* and the *o*.
5. In the original sentence's last word, change the second and third letters to *e* and *a*, respectively.

The new sentence is: *Leave the Navy in two years.*

Activity 9. Listening Well

Read the following ten directions to the students. Each set of directions consists of three parts. The first part is from column A, the second is from column B, and the third is from column C. Give students sufficient time to work out their answers. The students will record their responses on the activity 9 "Listening Well" page in this section. The correct answers are found in the answer key.

TEACHER'S DIRECTIONS

1. In the space next to the number 1, write down the name of the world's second largest continent, the highest prime number, and the word meaning "horrible" or "ghastly."
2. In the space following the number 2, write the name of the capital of the United States, the square of 3, and the word meaning "to start up trouble."
3. After number 3, record the name of the city nicknamed "The Big Apple," the number of years in a century, and the word meaning "to mark."
4. After number 4, write the name of the capital of Spain, the number that is 1/2 of 100, and the word meaning "to show off."
5. In the space next to the number 5, write the name of the southernmost North American city found in column A, the number that is a score, and the word meaning "to give up completely."
6. After number 6, write the name of the continent that contains the country of Argentina, the number of weeks in a year, and the word meaning "to make afraid."
7. Next to the number 7, record the name of the U.S. state consisting of a group of islands, the number that is 3⁄4's of 100, and the word meaning "to trouble or worry."
8. Beside number 8, write the name of the city that is the home of Big Ben, the number that is the lower prime number left in column B, and the word meaning "to go back and forth between choices."
9. In the space by number 9, write the name of the city in which the franc is prominent, the number that is 15% of 200, and the word meaning "to give out in shares."

10. In the space next to number 10, write the name of the U.S. city located near the Pacific Ocean, the number that is 1/9 of 27, and the word meaning "a haven or place of protection."

Activity 10. Methods to Improve Your Memory

After the students have had time to memorize the ten sentences found on the activity 10 "Methods to Improve Your Memory" page in this section, ask them the following ten questions. The answers follow.

TEACHER'S QUESTIONS

1. Who was appointed Secretary of the Treasury in 1789? (Alexander Hamilton)
2. Which English author completes the list of four read earlier? The authors are William Shakespeare, Charlotte Bronte, Charles Dickens, and _____ . (Jane Austen)
3. What is the only Ivy League school starting with the letter *D*? (Dartmouth)
4. Who was the MVP in the 1982 tournament in which North Carolina defeated Georgetown? (James Worthy)
5. Name four propaganda techniques in advertising. (testimonials, card stacking, name calling, and bandwagon approach)
6. Where is the National Academy of Science located? (2101 Constitution Avenue NW in Washington, D.C.)
7. Name the two mathematical figures that begin with the letter *r*. (rhombus and rectangle)
8. What is the name of the newspaper published in Los Angeles? (*Los Angeles Times*)
9. Name three of the six components of Bloom's Taxonomy. (knowledge, comprehension, application, analysis, synthesis, and evaluation)
10. Name the two animals beginning with the letter *c* that immigrated to South America. (cat and camel)

Activity 11. Memory Is a Good Tool

After the students have had time to memorize the ten sentences found on the activity 11 "Memory is a Good Tool" page in this section, ask them the following questions. Students may record their answers either orally or on a separate piece of paper. The answers are found after the questions.

TEACHER'S QUESTIONS

1. What did Billy do? (tumbled)
2. What did Marcia do? (stumbled)

3. Which team did not play? (Angels)

4. What sonata did Beethoven write? ("Moonlight")

5. Who wrote Rhapsody in E-Flat Major? (Brahms)

6. What time does "Seinfeld" start? (nine)

7. What show begins at eight? ("Star Trek")

8. Which road should the motorist look for after Sunrise Highway? (Washington Avenue)

9. What is the last road the motorist will be on? (Hicksville Road)

10. How many eggs does the recipe call for? (one)

11. How many minutes should the waffles stay in the waffle iron? (fifteen)

12. What does the student have to do for social studies regarding Africa? (do three pages of objective questions)

13. The student must do assignments from four different subjects. Name all four subjects. (biology, English, social studies, art)

14. Who rebounded Barkley's shot? (Robinson)

15. Who shot a three-pointer at the buzzer? (Stockton)

16. What directive is given after the directive, "Be quiet"? (Be loud.)

17. What is the last directive? (Be you.)

18. What one color is better than any combination? (yellow)

19. Which is worth more—two reds or four whites? (two reds)

20. Two greens are the same as two of what color? (orange)

Activity 12. Remembering the Order of People, Places, and Things

After the students have had time to memorize the items found in the ten sentences found on the activity 12 "Remembering the Order of People, Places, and Things" page in this section, ask them the following questions. They may respond orally or on a separate piece of paper. The answers are found after each question.

TEACHER'S QUESTIONS

1. Name three of the four favorite U.S. Presidents. (Franklin Roosevelt, Eisenhower, Hayes, Jefferson)

2. Which street that he drove past last Friday evening would be listed last if they were listed alphabetically? (Yale Court)

3. Which street would be listed first if they were listed alphabetically? (Fountain Street)

4. Which street is also the name of an Ivy League college? (Yale Court)

5. Which street is the name of an occupation? (Mechanic)

6. What period is his lunch period? (six)

7. Social studies is what period? (eight)

8. Which neighbor is *not* on his side of the street—McPhee, Kallback, O'Connor, or Tarantino? (O'Connor)

9. Which family *not* on his side of the street has a monosyllabic name? (Short)

10. Who plays baseball? (Ricky)

11. Which two work out? (Chris, Jim)

12. What does Kate do? (sings and acts)

13. What does Maureen do? (plays tennis)

14. Who wrote *Ethan Frome*? (Edith Wharton)

15. Name Nancy's two boys. (Mike, Gary)

16. Who is Kelly's mother? (Jill)

17. Who has three sisters? (Tom)

18. Who is Ellen's son? (James)

19. Who wore the white dress? (Priscilla)

20. What did Louise wear? (black evening gown)

21. Which lady wore the one-piece bathing suit? (Luanne)

22. Match these people with their occupations (Students will give the name after you've given the occupation.) retired executive . . . Jim; soda distributor . . . Tom; editor . . . Connie; marketing specialist . . . Gary; lawyer . . . John

23. Why does Jose have to see the mechanic? (car noise)

24. What has Jose borrowed that needs to be returned? (library books)

25. Where is the first place Jose said he has to go today? (cleaners)

Activity 15. Listen and Identify (Part One) and Activity 16. Listen and Identify (Part Two)

This game is a lot of fun for students. Break the class up into two equal groups, Team One and Team Two. Then break each team up into the Clue Givers and the Clue Receivers. Ask one Clue Giver and one Clue Receiver to sit in the two desks in the front of the room. The Clue Receiver's back is to the blackboard. The Clue Giver has the page entitled "Listen and Identify Part One" (or "Two") on his desk. Similar to the television show *Password*, the task of the Clue Givers is to give clues to the Clue Receivers in hopes that the Clue Receivers will be able to identify the word. These clues can be one-word clues, sentences, or anything in between. No bodily suggestions or hints are allowed. No part of the answer can be given in the clue(s). If it is, a point is deducted. A Clue Giver or Clue Receiver may elect to skip a word and move on to the next word; however, this will be a point deduction. Usually a time limit of 1 minute is fair for each pair of game participants. After the minute, count up the number of correct answers, subtract the deductions, and this number becomes that team's score. Move on to two members of the opposite team and do the same. When the next two players come to the front, they should pick up with the next word on that team's list. Keep a running tally of the scores of both Teams One and Two. When the game is played again, the students who were Clue Givers should be the Clue Receivers, and vice-versa.

It is important that the Clue Receivers do not see the words beforehand. One suggestion that is helpful for added excitement, but that will also take some time, is to have the Clue Givers print their words (answers) in big letters before the game starts, one word per page, and have another student hold each page up as the clues are given so that the other students can see the answer. Of course, the Clue Receiver should not be able to see this page at any time. In this way, the whole class, and not just the Clue Giver, can be in on the answer word. It's up to you. If the class completes the list, the students could compose more lists on their own and have more fun!

Activity 17. Hear, Remember, Repeat

Read the five sets of sentences to the students, one set at a time. The students will record their answers in the spaces provided on the activity 17 "Hear, Remember, Repeat" page in this section.

TEACHER'S SECTION

First set of sentences:
Mr. Kennedy has three dogs and two cats.
All three dogs are black, one cat is yellow, and one is gray.
He lives on Indiana Street between Hillman Drive and Willow Avenue.

Second set of sentences:
The largest state in the United States is Alaska, covering 570,833 square miles.
The smallest state in the country is Rhode Island, covering 1,055 square miles.
The state that is in the middle of the United States, in area, is Iowa.

Third set of sentences:
This summer we plan to go to Switzerland and Austria.
Last summer my grandparents from Italy visited us from June 29 to August 19.
My grandfather on my mother's side fought in World War II.

Fourth set of sentences:
John and Ellen own a Volvo.
Jim and Martha own a Dodge.
Gary and Nancy own a van.
Ray and Jill own a horse and buggy.

Fifth set of sentences:
My first period class is film study with Mrs. Daher.
My second period class is mathematics with Mr. Griffith.
My third period class is English with Mr. Pryal.
My fourth period class is art with Mr. Nepo.
My guidance counselor is Mr. Bencivenga.

Activity 18. Please Explain It to Me

Twelve topics are offered here. Select any topic(s) you feel your students would be able to handle and enjoy. The students will record their work in the space provided on the activity 18 "Please Explain It to Me" page in this section.

Here are some topics that your students might use:

1. How to play an instrument

2. How to throw a curve ball

3. How to get a kite up in the air

4. How to change a bicycle tire

5. How to make a French braid

6. How to properly serve a tennis ball

7. How to operate a machine (CD player, stereo, washer, etc.)

8. How to fix a mechanical problem

9. How to cook something

10. How to eat a healthy diet

11. How to read a chart

12. How to gather information for a report

Name _____ Date _____ Period _____

I. WRITING DIRECTIONS

Would you be able to tell someone how to get to your locker from the cafeteria and then how to open the locker and find your notebook? Could you direct someone who has never been to your house or apartment to get there from your school?

Here are several opportunities for you to show how well you can direct or instruct another person. On a separate piece of paper write as many of these as your teacher suggests.

Write the directions for:

1. How to go from your school to your house or apartment
2. How to tie your shoes
3. How to make a peanut butter and jelly sandwich if you have a knife, spoon, two slices of bread, an unopened jar of peanut butter, an unopened jar of jelly, a plate, and a napkin
4. How to change a bicycle's flat tire
5. How to program a VCR
6. How to play a particular instrument
7. How to get your mom or dad to agree to something that you think he or she might not initially agree to
8. How to brush your teeth properly

Name _____ Date _____ Period _____

2. STAND AND DELIVER

Please read all twenty sentences first. Then enjoy yourself and have some fun.

1. Write your last name on the line at the end of this sentence. _____

2. In the space after this sentence, write your birthday using only numbers, such as 11/2/85. _____

3. What number is missing here? Fill it in. 1, 2, 3, ___, 5.

4. Add your shoe size to the number 6 and write the total here. _____

5. Draw a box around your birthday in number 2 above.

6. On the reverse side of this page, draw two triangles of any size.

7. With your pen or pencil in your left hand, underline every word in this sentence.

8. Stand up next to your desk and count silently up to five.

9. Write down the exact time here. _____

10. Write down the letters of your favorite color here. _____

11. Tap your pen or pencil on your desk three times.

12. Stand up, slowly turn around, and then sit back down.

13. Raise both hands in the air and clap twice.

14. Say hello to the person in a seat near yours.

15. Write down the color of your teacher's shoes. _____

16. Unscramble these letters and write the correct word on the reverse side inside one of the triangles. (d b n e)

17. Tell a classmate your telephone number.

18. Stand up and jog in place for five seconds.

19. Write your favorite month on the chalkboard.

20. Now that you have read these other nineteen sentences, simply sign your name in the space below. Remain in your seat. Do none of the other directions on this page!

Name _____

TEACHER'S READING PAGE

3. AESOP'S "THE TWO TRAVELERS AND THE BEAR"

The Two Travelers and the Bear

Two friends were traveling along a road one day when, much to their surprise, a bear suddenly appeared. One of the travelers quickly left the other and climbed up a big, stout tree. The other was not so quick in his actions. Seeing that the bear would overtake him before he could hide, he lay down on the ground and pretended to be dead, because it is said that a bear will not touch a dead body. The bear poked him up and down, and then put its muzzle close to the man's ear for a moment. Eventually it ambled back into the woods. After it had gone away, the man who had fled up the tree climbed down and rejoined his companion. "Did the bear hurt you?" he asked. The other said, "No, he just whispered in my ear and left." While he was dusting himself off, his friend inquired, "What did the bear say to you?" "He told me," he replied, "to take care in future not to travel with friends who disappear at the first sign of danger."

A friend in need is a friend indeed.

TEACHER'S READING PAGE

4. CASEY AT THE BAT

ERNEST LAWRENCE THAYER

The outlook wasn't brilliant for the Mudville nine that day;
The score stood four to two with but one inning more to play.
And then when Cooney died at first, and Barrows did the same,
A sickly silence fell upon the patrons of the game.

A straggling few got up to go in deep despair. The rest
Clung to that hope which springs eternal in the human breast;
They thought if only Casey could but get a whack at that—
We'd put up even money now with Casey at the bat.

But Flynn preceded Casey, as did also Jimmy Blake,
And the former was a lulu and the latter was a cake;
So upon that stricken multitude grim melancholy sat,
For there seemed but little chance of Casey's getting to the bat.

But Flynn let drive a single, to the wonderment of all,
And Blake, the much despised, tore the cover off the ball;
And when the dust had lifted, and the men saw what had occurred,
There was Jimmy safe at second and Flynn a-hugging third.

Then from five thousand throats and more there rose a lusty yell;
It rumbled through the valley, it rattled in the dell;
It knocked upon the mountain and recoiled upon the flat,
For Casey, mighty Casey, was advancing to the bat.

There was ease in Casey's manner as he stepped into his place;
There was pride in Casey's bearing and a smile on Casey's face.
And when, responding to the cheers, he lightly doffed his hat,
No stranger in the crowd could doubt 'twas Casey at the bat.

Ten thousand eyes were on him as he rubbed his hands with dirt;
Five thousand tongues applauded when he wiped them on his shirt.
Then while the writhing pitcher ground the ball into his hip,
Defiance gleamed in Casey's eye, a sneer curled Casey's lip.

And now the leather-covered sphere came hurtling through the air,
And Casey stood a-watching it in haughty grandeur there.
Close by the sturdy batsman the ball unheeded sped—
"That ain't my style," said Casey. "Strike one," the umpire said.

From the benches, black with people, there went up a muffled roar,
Like the beating of the storm waves on a stern and distant shore.
"Kill him! Kill the umpire!" shouted someone on the stand;
And it's likely they'd have killed him had not Casey raised his hand.

With a smile of Christian charity great Casey's visage shone;
He stilled the rising tumult; he bade the game go on;
He signaled to the pitcher, and once more the spheroid flew;
But Casey still ignored it, and the umpire said, "Strike two."

"Fraud!" cried the maddened thousands, and echo answered, "Fraud!"
But one scornful look from Casey and the audience was awed.
They say his face grow stern and cold, they saw his muscles strain,
And they knew that Casey wouldn't let the ball go by again.

The sneer is gone from Casey's lip, his teeth are clenched in hate;
He pounds with cruel violence his bat upon the plate.
And now the pitcher holds the ball, and now he lets it go,
And now the air is shattered by the force of Casey's blow.

Oh, somewhere in this favored land the sun is shining bright;
The band is playing somewhere, and somewhere hearts are light,
And somewhere men are laughing, and somewhere children shout;
But there is no joy in Mudville—mighty Casey has struck out.

TEACHER'S READING PAGE

5. AGAMEMNON

Maybe we were mistaken to name
you after a warrior and expect you to be
content with just the taste of the
afternoon sun on your neck.

But you liked the preying, the pounce, a bird scratched dead,
making flesh welt and swell in thick pain
making grown men wince, true to your name.

Oh, Aggie, you were so small once,
could hide between Kafka and Virgil on my bookshelf
or lose yourself in the folds of my pillows, in the shapes of my dreams.

And I loved when I was reading something
awful, how you would come and lie on my chest
and we would breathe together in the same, easy rhythm.

Your first kill was a mouse
and you brought it inside to show us all
because you were so proud and we didn't much mind
because mice are so dreadful and you so dear.
And I think we rewarded you with some Meow Mix
and maybe a bowl of milk because catching
mice is what you were meant to do.

And, Aggie, I cried when we drove you there
and you whined with each turn of the wheel and you looked
as though you knew exactly where you were going.

Mother handed you to the vet and they asked
if we wanted to hold your hand. I felt like
Clytemnestra in the bathtub, how she held
that knife in her hand and stabbed and stabbed and stabbed
and how he bled all over because
he had been so wrong and so bad and so evil and how
you really weren't and I told them
that I didn't need to watch.

They told me that
they would take care of your body,
that I needn't worry about it.
All I could think of was that
time that I thought you were dead
when I saw a grey cat on the side of
the road and his face was all bloody and wrong
and I cried and cried at the roadside
because it was such a hot day,
such a violently awful death.
At home you were lying on the couch,
lazy eyes rolling,
and someone else was worrying about that cat.
Tonight, you fall gently into sleep
and I am wondering which death is worse.

And I am wondering if Clytemnestra hated
herself afterwards as she stood there
with that knife. Or if maybe, she smiled, laughed,
went back to the warm arms of her lover.

I walk to the car, don't speak,
go home to a house that is easy to walk in
but is screaming your absence.

—*Celeste Perri*

Agamemnon: king of Mycenae and commander in chief of the Greek army in the Trojan War, killed by his wife, Clytemnestra.

Name _____ Date _____ Period _____

6. ACCIDENT'S HAPPEN!

Listen carefully as your teacher reads an accident account. Then answer the questions as completely as possible.

1. What day of the week did the accident happen? _____
2. What season of the year was it? _____
3. Which driver was in a Cemmo? _____
4. Who drove the Hall Lion? _____
5. Who was heading west? _____
6. Who was driving in a southerly direction? _____
7. Who was driven in a direction perpendicular to Mr. Manning? _____
8. What is The Manor? _____
9. In what town did the accident occur? _____
10. Who was driving parallel to Manning? _____
11. What decade in life is Ms. Masterson? _____
12. How many years separate Jackson and Manning? _____
13. Which words in the article mean that Neilson thought he did not have to stop? _____
14. Was the left or right side of Masterson's car damaged by the initial impact with Neilson's car? _____
15. Who has a broken leg? _____
16. Who definitely required stitches? _____
17. What does the word "impounded" mean? _____
18. What is an abrasion? _____
19. Which person seems to have been hurt the most? _____
20. How did Manning's car get damaged? _____

7. DOES IT LOOK THE SAME?

After your teacher has read each direction, do what is asked of you in the space below. Then when all the directions have been completed, compare your results with the original. Be sure to listen closely and follow the directions accurately.

Name _____ Date _____ Period _____

8. LISTEN AND MAKE THE CHANGES

Here are four sentences that will change before your very eyes to four completely different sentences. Listen to the changes read by your teacher and use the work space to make the corrections. Then write the new sentences in the spaces provided.

1. The boat is very huge.

Work Space: _____

New Sentence: _____

2. The flower arrangement is noted.

Work Space: _____

New Sentence: _____

3. He will break the track record.

Work Space: _____

New Sentence: _____

4. Sieve the gravy into yours.

Work Space: _____

New Sentence: _____

9. LISTENING WELL

Follow the directions read by your teacher. In the spaces below, record each answer in its proper order.

COLUMN A	COLUMN B	COLUMN C
Africa	1	abandon
Hawaii	3	allot
London	9	brand
Los Angeles	20	flaunt
Madrid	29	grisly
Miami	30	harass
New York City	50	instigate
Paris	52	intimidate
South America	75	shelter
Washington, D.C.	100	waver

1. _____
2. _____
3. _____
4. _____
5. _____
6. _____
7. _____
8. _____
9. _____
10. _____

Name _____ Date _____ Period _____

IO. METHODS TO IMPROVE YOUR MEMORY

Not only in school, but also in life outside the classroom, your memory is a good tool to help you to succeed in many ways. Whether it is remembering names, addresses, phone numbers, associations, or other similar tasks, your memory is quite important. Strategies or tactics to help improve your ability to recall facts, figures, and names are many. ROYGBIV is one mnemonic to recall the colors of the spectrum.

This activity asks you to use your personal memory helpers to help you recall these facts from different subjects. Your teacher will ask you questions based on the information on this page. Now concentrate well!

1. Alexander Hamilton was appointed Secretary of the Treasury in 1789.
2. The National Academy of Sciences is located at 2101 Constitution Avenue NW in Washington, D.C.
3. Some of the propaganda techniques in advertising include testimonials, card stacking, name calling, and bandwagon approaches.
4. The eight Ivy League colleges are Brown, Cornell, Harvard, Princeton, Yale, Pennsylvania, Columbia, and Dartmouth.
5. Seven basic mathematical figures are the circle, the rhombus, the square, the rectangle, the parallelogram, the triangle, and the trapezoid.
6. Famous English authors include William Shakespeare, Charles Dickens, Jane Austen, D. H. Lawrence, and Charlotte Bronte.
7. North American animal families that immigrated to South America are these: bear, camel, cat, deer, dog, and horse.
8. Some of the most widely read American newspapers include the *Wall Street Journal, USA Today,* the *Los Angeles Times,* the *New York Times,* and the *Washington Post.*
9. In 1982 Dean Smith's North Carolina Tar Heels defeated John Thompson's Georgetown Hoyas by the score of 63–62. James Worthy was the tournament MVP.
10. Bloom's Taxonomy includes knowledge, comprehension, application, analysis, synthesis, and evaluation.

II. MEMORY IS A GOOD TOOL

Memorize the items found in these ten sentences. Then answer the questions your teacher will ask you concerning the names and items found in these sentences. Good Luck!

1. George grumbled, Billy tumbled, Larry bumbled, and Marcia stumbled.

2. The Yankees won, the Tigers lost, the Angels did not play.

3. Bach wrote "The Well-Tempered Clavichord," Brahms wrote "Rhapsody in E-Flat Major," Beethoven wrote the "Moonlight" sonata.

4. "Jeopardy" starts at seven, "Wheel of Fortune" starts at seven-thirty, "Star Trek" starts at eight, "Seinfeld" starts at nine, and "ER" starts at ten.

5. Take Sunrise Highway east for about two miles until you see the sign for Washington Avenue. Turn left at the light, go past the railroad tracks and keep heading north for about seven blocks until you come to Clarke Street. Make a right here. Continue on Clarke and look for the fork in the road where you will bear left. Take that to Hicksville Road.

6. Use two cups of Frenchy's Baking Mix, one and one-third cups of milk, one egg, and two tablespoons of vegetable oil. Pour into a hot waffle iron. The waffles will be ready in approximately 15 minutes.

7. I have thirteen pages of biology to read, an essay about *Romeo and Juliet* for English, three pages of objective questions about Africa for social studies, and an art project all due tomorrow.

8. Johnson stole the ball and passed it to Barkley whose shot was rebounded by Robinson. Robinson was fouled as his shot was good for two points. He missed his foul shot. Malone rebounded it and passed to Stockton who hit a three pointer at the buzzer.

9. Be kind. Be one of a kind. Be quiet. Be loud. Be intelligent. Be silly. Be mindful. Be mindless. Be you.

10. Two reds are better than four whites. One blue is less than one black. Three greens are the same as two oranges. A single yellow is better than any combination.

Copyright © 1996 by John Wiley & Sons, Inc.

12. REMEMBERING THE ORDER OF PEOPLE, PLACES, AND THINGS

Here is a challenge for your mind. Memorize these ten sentences. Your teacher will then read a series of questions concerning items found within the sentences. Using the information you remember from these sentences, answer as completely as possible.

1. My four favorite U.S. presidents are Franklin Roosevelt, Dwight Eisenhower, Rutherford Hayes, and Thomas Jefferson.

2. I drove my car past these streets last Friday evening: Mechanic Street, Mansfield Drive, Yale Court, Scholar Court, and Fountain Street.

3. Here is my schedule: Period One, chemistry; Period Two, math; Period Three, gym; Period Four, free; Period Five, English; Period Six, lunch; Period Seven, Spanish; Period Eight, social studies.

4. Here are the names of the neighbors on my side of the street: Kallback, McPhee, Gavigan, and Tarantino. On the other side are the following families: Short, O'Connor, and Murphy.

5. For their enjoyment Martha gardens, Ricky plays baseball, Tommy plays basketball, Kate sings and acts, Maureen plays tennis, Chris and Jim work out, Gary coaches, and Ray boats. Grandpa John says he will start biking soon.

6. I have read these books during the last two years: *Catcher in the Rye* by J.D. Salinger, *Tom Sawyer* by Mark Twain, *An American Tragedy* by Theodore Dreiser, and *Ethan Frome* by Edith Wharton.

7. Nancy's two sons are Mike and Gary, Jill's daughter is Kelly, Ellie's son is James, Tom's children are Megan, Tom, Meredith, and Christine, and Judy's children are Dan, Emily, and Allison.

8. John wore a blue suit, Priscilla had on a white dress, Louise sported a black evening gown, and Luanne donned a one-piece bathing suit.

9. John is a lawyer, Jim is a retired executive, Ray is a photographer, Connie is an editor, Tom is a soda distributor, and Gary is a marketing specialist.

10. Today Jose has to drop off clothes at the cleaners, make a dental appointment, return books to the library, get a video, and see a mechanic about the noise his car is making.

Name _____ Date _____ Period _____

13. GREAT IN EIGHT (PART ONE)

Can you describe a person, place, or thing in eight or fewer words? This activity will test your ability to be both concise and accurate. Write your eight clues or describers next to the word in column A. After you have finished writing the clues, read them to your partner and see how many he or she can identify. Score one point for each correct response. An example is done for you.

Mississippi River: *long body of water in middle America; Twain*

COLUMN A

1. tooth: _____

2. flag: _____

3. mud: _____

4. turtle: _____

5. music: _____

6. movies: _____

7. plum: _____

8. cassette player: _____

9. circle: _____

10. whale: _____

11. barbells: _____

12. hair: _____

13. Alice in Wonderland: _____

14. July 4: _____

15. microphone: _____

Name _____ Date _____ Period _____

I4. GREAT IN EIGHT (PART TWO)

Can you describe a person, place, or thing in eight or fewer words? This activity will test your ability to be both concise and accurate. Write your clues or describers next to the word in column A. After you have finished writing the clues, read them to your partner and see how many he or she can identify. Score one point for each correct response. An example is done for you.

Mississippi River: long body of water in middle America; Twain

COLUMN A

1. Sylvester Stallone: _____

2. cheek: _____

3. England: _____

4. elbow: _____

5. stoplight: _____

6. grease: _____

7. roller coaster: _____

8. mathematics: _____

9. Santa Claus: _____

10. wheel: _____

11. August: _____

12. zero: _____

13. snake: _____

14. tea: _____

15. whistling: _____

Name _____ Date _____ Period _____

15. LISTEN AND IDENTIFY (PART ONE)

Your teacher has read the rules to you. Now have some fun!

1. Abraham Lincoln	21. rap music	41. sled
2. desk	22. mascara	42. comb
3. traffic jams	23. muscles	43. belt buckle
4. height	24. cookies	44. San Francisco
5. spaghetti	25. mildew	45. dictionary
6. doughnut	26. motorcycle	46. lamp
7. teens	27. prime number	47. swimming pool
8. television	28. bridge	48. wig
9. thumb	29. neck	49. ear wax
10. claustrophobia	30. heel	50. shore
11. lifeguard	31. elevator	51. Michael Jordan
12. Elvis Presley	32. dental floss	52. freezer
13. loneliness	33. graduation	53. kimono
14. weather	34. Disneyland	54. ghosts
15. handwriting	35. igloo	55. loitering
16. Thomas Edison	36. alligator	56. Boston Red Sox
17. clarinet	37. shelf	57. Louisiana
18. truck	38. ground	58. war
19. fortune cookie	39. police	59. airport
20. float	40. skipping	60. turkey

16. LISTEN AND IDENTIFY (PART TWO)

Now that you are familiar with the rules, enjoy yourselves and have some fun!

1. pickle
2. David Letterman
3. broom
4. tire
5. pool
6. skiing
7. New York City
8. jail
9. bookstore
10. flower
11. corner
12. computer
13. hamburger
14. basketball
15. pencil
16. globe
17. model
18. Humpty Dumpty
19. gym
20. Coca-Cola

21. tomato
22. mail
23. sunglasses
24. repair
25. barking
26. ice cream
27. cheerleader
28. wealth
29. telephone
30. taxi
31. dancing
32. inch
33. medal
34. snow
35. milk
36. sister
37. subway
38. religion
39. rabbit
40. machine

41. MTV
42. report card
43. mall
44. necklace
45. vacation
46. London
47. father
48. 2000
49. CD
50. yodel
51. toothpaste
52. *The Sound of Music*
53. guitar
54. jury
55. baby
56. weight lifter
57. orange
58. detention
59. staircase
60. lips

Name _____ Date _____ Period _____

17. HEAR, REMEMBER, REPEAT

Hearing names, actions, dates, and other information can be difficult at times. This activity will help to improve your listening and recall abilities. Your teacher will read a few sets of three sentences. After each set, write down any pertinent information you remember in the spaces provided, and then be ready to move on to your teacher's reading of four and then five sentences in a row. Your goal is to repeat as much of the original sentences as possible.

First set of sentences: _____

_____

_____

Second set of sentences: _____

_____

_____

Third set of sentences: _____

_____

_____

Fourth set of sentences: _____

_____

_____

Fifth set of sentences: _____

_____

_____

18. PLEASE EXPLAIN IT TO ME

This is your opportunity to explain to one of your classmates how to do something. In turn, your classmate will explain to you how to do something. Listen carefully to what you are told and then write what you have heard. Your classmate will do the same after your explanation. Your teacher will read a list of possibilities.

_____

_____

_____

_____

_____

_____

_____

_____

_____

_____

_____

_____

_____

_____

_____

_____

Section Two

ACROSS THE CURRICULUM

TEACHER DIRECTIONS TO SECTION TWO: ACROSS THE CURRICULUM

Activity 25. Social Studies Guess Who I Am Game

Read one clue at a time. If a student answers correctly after one clue, score three points. If he answers correctly after two clues, score two points. If he answers correctly after three, score one point. The answers are given after the third clue you read. Students will record your clues and their answers on the page entitled "25. Social Studies Guess Who I Am Game" in this section.

TEACHER'S SECTION

1. Born in 1860, I was elected to Congress in 1890 and 1892.

   Known for my oratory skills, I delivered my famous "Cross of Gold" speech at the 1896 Democratic Convention in Chicago.

   I lost the race for the U.S. presidency three times.

   (William Jennings Bryan)

2. I was a West Point graduate, a hero in the Mexican War, and a U.S. senator.

   After serving as Franklin Pierce's Secretary of War, I was later chosen president of the Confederacy.

   I was captured by the Union forces in 1865, imprisoned, and charged with treason. Though the charges were later dropped, I never regained my citizenship.

   (Jefferson Davis)

3. Born in 1813, I was known for my powers of oratory.

   A leader of the Democratic party, I was very vocal on the subject of slavery.

   I am most famous for my debates with Abraham Lincoln. I defeated Lincoln for the 1858 Illinois Senate seat.

   (Stephen Douglas)

4. My roles were many—printer, publisher, author, inventor, diplomat, and scientist.

   I invented a stove, bifocals, and a clock.

   I'm probably best remembered for my *Poor Richard's Almanack* and working with a kite and electricity.

   (Ben Franklin)

5. I was the first U.S. Secretary of the Treasury.

   I championed strong central government.

   I was killed in a duel with Aaron Burr.

   (Alexander Hamilton)

6. Born in 1737, I was the first governor of Massachusetts.

   I was a famous American Revolutionary leader.

   I was a "big" signer of the Declaration of Independence.

   (John Hancock)

7. I led the Texas war of independence against Mexico.

   I was elected president of the Republic of Texas and later became that state's senator and governor.

   A major city in Texas is named after me.

   (Sam Houston)

8. I was born into a famous New England family in 1925.

   A U.S. senator from New York, I successfully managed my brother's presidential campaign.

   While campaigning for my own presidential nomination, I was shot and killed in Los Angeles in 1968.

   (Robert F. Kennedy)

9. I was born into the Little family in 1925.

   A black separatist leader, I was associated with the Black Muslims.

   In 1965 I was assassinated while making a speech in New York.

   (Malcolm X)

10. I was a Sioux Indian leader born around 1831.

    An advocate of the Ghost Dance movement, I was arrested and later killed.

    My forces defeated George Custer at Little Big Horn.

    (Sitting Bull)

Activity 31. Listen and Spell

Please dictate these sentences to the students. The word they are asked to spell in each sentence is underlined. Students will record their answers on the page entitled "31. Listen and Spell" in this section.

TEACHER'S SECTION

1. Will this underline{affect} my final grade?
2. The groundskeepers at the golf underline{course} did a good job on the greens.
3. She was very thankful for your underline{counsel} that helped solve her problems.
4. Have you ever heard her give another person a underline{compliment}?
5. Everybody dressed underline{formally} for the prom.
6. The dove is the symbol of underline{peace}.

7. The team's <u>morale</u> was quite low after the devastating loss to our rival school.

8. Fran <u>led</u> us to the haunted house last night.

9. Ursula <u>passed</u> out after running so fast.

10. It was as <u>plain</u> as can be.

11. Do you think <u>they're</u> going to the concert with the others?

12. What is the <u>principal</u> cause of their unhappiness?

13. I would like to see <u>their</u> report.

14. <u>Whose</u> bike was left out in the rain?

15. This was certainly not a <u>waste</u> of time.

16. Tom <u>threw</u> the frisbee to his friend on the beach.

17. He did not feel <u>weak</u> after the strenuous exercises.

18. How many assistant <u>principals</u> are there in this school?

19. Her dad bought a box of white <u>stationery</u>.

20. We will meet <u>here</u> at ten o'clock.

21. Georgia was able to <u>piece</u> it together.

22. Roger and Justine are on the student <u>council</u>.

23. We felt <u>altogether</u> exhausted after the marathon dance contest.

24. Are <u>there</u> any more grapes left in the refrigerator?

25. Ken's brother makes delicious <u>desserts</u>.

26. We walked down the <u>aisle</u> slowly.

27. Jose usually gives intelligent <u>advice</u>.

28. The teacher showed us how to use the car <u>brakes</u>.

29. The woman <u>shoocd</u> the animal away.

30. When will they <u>board</u> the plane?

Activity 42. Potpourri Guess Me in Three Clues Game

See the directions for activity 25. Students will record your clues and their answers on the page entitled "42. Potpourri Guess Me in Three Clues Game" in this section.

TEACHER'S SECTION

1. I was born in Stratford-upon-Avon in England in 1564.
   I am known as the Bard.
   My works include *Hamlet*, *Romeo and Juliet*, and *Macbeth*.
   (William Shakespeare)

2. I was born in 1895 and raised in Baltimore, Maryland.
   They say I built a house in the Bronx, New York.
   I hit a total of 714 major league home runs.
   (Babe Ruth)

3. I lived at 221-B Baker Street in London.
   People thought I was killed off, but Doyle wouldn't allow it.
   My companion was Dr. Watson.
   (Sherlock Holmes)

4. I was command pilot of *Gemini 8* in 1966.
   In 1969 I said, "That's one small step for a man, one giant leap for mankind."
   I was the first man to walk on the moon.
   (Neil Armstrong)

5. I was a Rhodes Scholar.
   My native state is Arkansas.
   I succeeded George Bush as U.S. president.
   (Bill Clinton)

6. I am best-known by my first name.
   In 1805 I defeated Russia and Austria at Austerlitz.
   I was defeated at Waterloo in 1815.
   (Napoleon Bonaparte)

7. I led a 382-day boycott that eventually brought about a Supreme Court decision regarding segregation.
   I won the Nobel Peace Prize in 1964.
   I was assassinated in Memphis, Tennessee, in 1968.
   (Martin Luther King Jr.)

8. I lived for ninety years during the nineteenth and twentieth centuries.
   I was a nurse and spy for the Union Army in the Civil War.
   I led the Underground Railroad.
   (Harriet Tubman)

9. Raised in Liverpool, England, I was killed in New York City in 1980.
   My son and wife also had recording careers.
   I was the composer of many of the Beatles hits.
   (John Lennon)

10. I was an Italian navigator and explorer.
    I was greatly helped by Ferdinand and Isabella.
    Americans celebrate a holiday in my honor in October.
    (Christopher Columbus)

Activity 43. English Class Guess Which Author I Am Game

See the directions for activity 25. Students will record your clues and their answers on the page entitled "43. English Class Guess Which Author I Am Game" in this section.

TEACHER'S SECTION

1. I supposedly was a Phrygian slave who lived mostly in the sixth century B.C.

   My stories depict animal characters who behave and speak as if they were human beings.

   Each of my stories ends with a moral.

   (Aesop)

2. I was born in Landport, England, in 1812 and worked in a blacking factory as a child.

   My father was imprisoned for debts he owed.

   My most read writings include "A Christmas Carol," *David Copperfield*, *Oliver Twist*, and *A Tale of Two Cities*.

   (Charles Dickens)

3. I graduated from Edinburgh, Scotland University's School of Medicine and began my medical practice in England.

   Some of my writings include "The Red Headed League" and *The Hound of the Baskervilles*.

   I created the world's most famous detective.

   (Sir Arthur Conan Doyle)

4. My grandfather was a judge in the Salem, Massachusetts, witchcraft trials.

   I attended Bowdoin College with Franklin Pierce and Henry Wadsworth Longfellow.

   I wrote *The House of the Seven Gables* and *The Scarlet Letter*.

   (Nathaniel Hawthorne)

5. I'm better known by my pen name than I am by my real name, William Sydney Porter.

   I am best known for my portraits of city life and my stories' ironic endings.

   People seemed to love my short story, "The Gift of the Magi."

   (O. Henry)

6. An American, I went to sea at seventeen and later joined the Gold Rush.

   I was also a news correspondent in the Russo-Japanese War.

My most famous writings include *The Call of the Wild* and *The Sea Wolf*.
(Jack London)

7. I created the world's most famous whale.

    My first novels dealt with adventure and travel.

    The first line of my most famous novel begins with "Call me Ishmael."
    (Herman Melville)

8. Both of my parents were actors who died when I was three.

    When I was twenty-seven, I married my thirteen-year-old cousin, Virginia Clemm.

    Credit me with "The Raven" and "The Pit and the Pendulum."
    (Edgar Allan Poe)

9. I was born in Salinas, California, in 1902 and made that area the setting for some of my writings.

    My writings include *The Red Pony* and *The Grapes of Wrath*.

    I also created the mentally deficient Lennie Small and his friend, George Wilson, in the novel, *Of Mice and Men*.
    (John Steinbeck)

10. I probably made the Mississippi River more famous than any other author did.

    I was born and died in the same year that Halley's Comet appeared, 1835 and 1910.

    My most famous creations were Tom and Huck.
    (Mark Twain—Samuel Langhorne Clemens)

Activity 46. The Science Guess Who I Am Game

See the directions for activity 25. Students will record your clues and their answers on the page entitled "46. The Science Guess Who I Am Game" in this section.

TEACHER'S SECTION

1. Born in 1864, I was a botanist best known for my work in the area of agriculture.

    The son of slaves, I attended Tuskegee Institute in Alabama.

    My major contribution to the farmers dealt with peanuts and sweet potatoes.
    (George Washington Carver)

2. A polish-born French physicist, I discovered radium.

    I won the Nobel prize for physics in 1903 and for chemistry in 1911.

    I was assisted by my husband, Pierre, while researching radium.
    (Marie Curie)

3. A British naturalist born in 1809, I originated the theory of evolution.

My most famous writing is entitled *On the Origin of Species*.

People remember me by the phrase, "the survival of the fittest."

(Charles Darwin)

4. I am credited with more than 1,000 inventions.

   An American, I was given the name "The Wizard of Menlo Park."

   I invented the microphone, the phonograph, the stock ticker, and the incandescent light bulb.

   (Thomas Edison)

5. A German-born American theoretical physicist, I proposed the theory of relativity.

   I won the Nobel prize for physics in 1921.

   Element #99 on the periodic table is named after me.

   (Albert Einstein)

6. I was an Austrian physician born in 1856.

   I developed a theory of neurosis and the psychoanalytic technique of free association.

   My most important work is entitled *The Interpretation of Dreams*.

   (Sigmund Freud)

7. Born in 1564, I was a mathematician, physicist, and astronomer.

   I preferred scientific experimentation and systematic observation over philosophical speculation.

   After my trial as a proponent of the Copernican theory of a sun-centered universe, I said, "And yet it moves," as I referred to the earth's movement around the sun.

   (Galilei Galileo)

8. I was an English physician born in 1578.

   My patients included Sir Francis Bacon, James I, and Charles I.

   I'm most famous for my discoveries dealing with the circulation of blood.

   (William Harvey)

9. An English physicist and mathematician, I was born about the middle of the seventeenth century.

   I discovered the binomial theorem, calculus, and the reflecting telescope.

   In my writing, *Principia*, I explained the law of gravitation.

   (Sir Isaac Newton)

10. A French chemist born in 1822, I studied the subject of fermentation.

    While working in Paris, I treated diseases such as yellow fever, plague, and cholera with vaccines.

    I am the founder of the science of bacteriology.

    (Louis Pasteur)

19. THE WHO, THE WHAT, THE WHERE

Twelve events from American history are recounted in this activity. Although the dates of the events are correct, the people or the places associated with these events are mixed up. Select the correct name from the columns below the last event, and write it's letter in the proper space within the sentence. Each name is used only once.

1. January 10, 1876 _____ forms The _____ in Ohio.

2. February 3, 1959 _____ and _____ are killed in a plane crash in _____.

3. March 30, 1981 _____ is shot outside the _____ by _____.

4. April 22, 1864 The phrase "_____" begins to be incorporated on U.S. currency.

5. May 30, 1922 The _____ is dedicated in Washington, D.C.

6. June 16, 1858 _____ states, "A house divided against itself cannot stand."

7. July 23, 1984 _____ becomes the first _____ to resign.

8. August 7, 1782 _____ establishes the _____ as a badge of military merit.

9. September 8, 1974 _____ pardons former President _____.

10. October 26, 1865 The _____ opens.

11. November 12, 1983 The _____ doll is created.

12. December 19, 1732 _____ publishes _____ in Philadelphia.

(a) Ames, Iowa
(b) Cabbage Patch
(c) Erie Canal
(d) President Ford
(e) Benjamin Franklin
(f) John W. Hinckley
(g) Buddy Holly
(h) In God We Trust
(i) Lincoln
(j) Lincoln Memorial

(k) Miss America
(l) Poor Richard's Almanack
(m) Purple Heart
(n) Richard Nixon
(o) President Reagan
(p) John D. Rockefeller
(q) Standard Oil Company
(r) Ritchie Valens
(s) George Washington
(t) Washington Hilton Hotel
(u) Vanessa Williams

20. PUTTING THE EVENTS OF THE TWENTIETH CENTURY TOGETHER

This exercise is a tough one. You are asked to arrange the events in each group in sequential order. The tough part is that they all happened between 1921 and 1982, a short period of history. If you have done both groups correctly, the letters preceding each statement will spell out the last names of two famous people of the twentieth century.

GROUP ONE

E. President Richard Nixon resigns.

N. Martin Luther King is killed in Memphis, Tennessee.

Y. The nation's first major nuclear disaster occurs in Pennsylvania.

D. Woodrow Wilson dies in his sleep.

S. President Kennedy is killed by a sniper in Dallas.

I. Lindberg flies to Paris in 33 ½ hours.

The famous twentieth century person is __ __ __ __ __ __ .

GROUP TWO

A. Babe Ruth hits 60 homers in a single season.

V. Barney Clark receives first artificial heart transplant.

M. Vietnam Accord is reached; Cease-fire is to begin.

S. The stock market collapses.

O. Carter defeats Ford.

I. Men walk on the moon.

The famous twentieth century person is __ __ __ __ __ __ .

43

21. WHAT THE QUOTE MEANS TO ME

Here are eight quotes from famous people who lived at different times. Each quote has something of importance to teach us. In the space provided write what the quote means to you. If time, discuss your responses with your classmates.

1. "This above all—to thine own self be true;
   And it must follow, as the night the day,
   Thou canst not then be false to any man." (Shakespeare)

   _____

   _____

2. "Tis better to have loved and lost
   Than never to have loved at all." (Tennyson)

   _____

   _____

3. "Beauty without expression tires." (Emerson)

   _____

   _____

4. "The true use of speech is not so much to express our wants as to conceal them." (Goldsmith)

   _____

   _____

5. "To be proud with knowledge is to be blind with light." (Franklin)

   _____

   _____

6. "Truth is mighty and will prevail. There is the matter with this, except that it ain't so." (Twain)

   _____

   _____

7. "Do not seek death. Death will find you. But seek the road which makes death a fulfillment." (Hammarskjöld)

   _____

   _____

21. WHAT THE QUOTE MEANS TO ME, CONTINUED

8. "Deep in the cavern of the infant's breast,
   The father's nature lurks, and lives anew." (Horace)

   _____

   _____

9. "And when the One Great Scorer comes
      to mark against your name,
   He writes not that you won or lost—
      But how you played the game." (Grantland Rice)

   _____

   _____

10. "We must open the doors of opportunity. But we
    must equip people to walk through those doors." (Lyndon B. Johnson)

    _____

    _____

22. TIME MARCHES ON

If you have arranged the events in each group in the correct chronological order, you will have spelled out a message concerning loyalty. Write the correct letter sequence in the spaces below each group to find out the message.

N. Jesus is crucified.

E. Julius Caesar is murdered by Brutus, Cassius, and others.

R. Homer writes the *Iliad* and the *Odyssey*.

S. Muhammad dies.

I. Alexander the Great dies.

F. King Tut reigns in Egypt.

D. Jutes, Angles, and Saxons invade Britain.

— — — — — — —

P. Kublai Khan becomes ruler of the Mongol Empire.

H. Charlemagne is born.

L. First Crusade begins.

E. Eric the Red founds colonies in Greenland.

— — — —

A. Michelangelo paints the Sistine Chapel.

E. Joan of Arc is burned at the stake.

C. Spanish Armada is defeated.

H. *Mayflower* lands.

— — — —

E. American Civil War.

O. Seven Years' War begins.

R. The Wright brothers fly their airplane.

T. Boston Massacre takes place.

H. Napoleon is crowned emperor of France.

— — — — —

The message is:

— — — — — — —   — — — —   — — — —   — — — — —.

Name _____ Date _____ Period _____

23. FRACTURED HEADLINES

At the bottom of the page, write the letters that complete the sentences begun in Group One about these events in history. Take a letter from each group (two through four) to complete the sentences.

GROUP ONE

(A) Alaska joins
(B) The National League
(C) The Federal Government approves AZT
(D) The Whig Party
(E) JFK
(F) George Washington is chosen

GROUP TWO

(G) the 35th president of the U.S.
(H) in the treatment
(I) the Union
(J) is established
(K) becomes
(L) Commander-in-Chief

GROUP THREE

(M) the first professional baseball league
(N) by opponents of Andrew Jackson
(O) of AIDS patients
(P) is born in Brookline, Massachusetts
(Q) as the 49th state
(R) of the Continental Army

GROUP FOUR

(S) on June 15, 1775.   (V) on May 29, 1917.
(T) on April 14, 1834.   (W) on January 3, 1959.
(U) on February 2, 1876.   (X) on March 20, 1987.

A _ _ _   D   _ _ _
B _ _ _   E   _ _ _
C _ _ _   F   _ _ _

47

24. MORE FRACTURED HEADLINES

At the bottom of the page, write the letters that complete the sentences begun in Group One about these events in history. Take a letter from each group (two through four) to complete the sentences.

GROUP ONE

(A) Elvis Presley
(B) The Nineteenth Amendment is enacted
(C) California
(D) Thurgood Marshall
(E) The American Embassy in Iran
(F) Philadelphia

GROUP TWO

(G) becomes the first Black
(H) giving women
(I) becomes
(J) of Mississippi
(K) is seized
(L) joins the Union

GROUP THREE

(M) Supreme Court Justice
(N) makes his first record
(O) as the 31st state
(P) and 65 hostages are taken
(Q) the right to vote
(R) the capital of the United States

GROUP FOUR

(S) on October 2, 1967.
(T) on September 9, 1850.
(U) on December 6, 1790.
(V) on July 6, 1954.
(W) on August 26, 1920.
(X) on November 4, 1979.

A __ __ __   D __ __ __
B __ __ __   E __ __ __
C __ __ __   F __ __ __

25. SOCIAL STUDIES GUESS WHO I AM GAME

Your teacher will read a series of clues concerning ten famous Americans. Select particular words or phrases that help you to identify each person. Record the clues, answers, and points in the spaces provided.

1. _____ _____ _____
   Answer: _____ Points: _____

2. _____ _____ _____
   Answer: _____ Points: _____

3. _____ _____ _____
   Answer: _____ Points: _____

4. _____ _____ _____
   Answer: _____ Points: _____

5. _____ _____ _____
   Answer: _____ Points: _____

6. _____ _____ _____
   Answer: _____ Points: _____

7. _____ _____ _____
   Answer: _____ Points: _____

8. _____ _____ _____
   Answer: _____ Points: _____

9. _____ _____ _____
   Answer: _____ Points: _____

10. _____ _____ _____
   Answer: _____ Points: _____

The total number of points accumulated is _____ .

26. THE WORDS (IN LETTERS) OF FAMOUS AMERICANS

Here are the words of ten famous quotes by ten famous Americans. Unfortunately, only the first letters of the quotes are given to you and the last names of the speakers have been scrambled up after the quote. In the space provided, write the words of the quote and the speaker's name after the quote.

1. F A S Y A .   (ILNLOCN)

_____

2. G M L O G M D.   (EHRYN)

_____

3. I H A D!   (NKGI)

_____

4. A N W Y C C D F Y: A W Y C D F Y C.   (NEYEKDN)

_____

5. I C T A L.   (SHWNTANGOI)

_____

6. R M L! N N T!   (HUBS)

_____

7. I Y C S T H, G O O T K.   (RMTAUN)

_____

8. T A T T T T M S.   (ANPIE)

_____

9. Y W H D N T K A A.   (XNOIN)

_____

10. T B S H!   (TAURNM)

_____

27. THE ABC'S OF GEOGRAPHY

With a little help from a country's location and its first and last letters, you're challenged to identify these countries that are listed alphabetically. Fill in the country's missing letters. Unscramble the circled letters and you have the names of two famous world explorers. Write their names after the last country.

1. A __ __ __ __ __ __ __ a: large country in southern South America

2. (B)__ __ __ __ l: largest country in South America

3. C __ __ (○)e: the western coast of southern South America

4. D __ __ __ __ __ k: northern Europe between the North and Baltic Seas

5. E __ __ __ __ __ __ __ a: east of Sudan in East Africa

6. F __ __ __ (○)__ d: in northern Europe

7. G __ __ __ __ e: on the Balkan peninsula in southeast Europe

8. H __ __ __ i: on the island of Hispaniola in the West Indies

9. I __ __ (○)__ __ d: on the north end of the Atlantic Ocean

10. J __ __ __ __ __ n: east of Israel and north of Saudi Arabia

11. K __ __ __ a: on the Indian Ocean coast of East Africa

12. L __ __ __ __ __ __ __ (○)__ __ __ n: small country in the Alps

13. M __ __ __ (○)o: between Central America and the United States

14. N __ __ __ __ y: on the Scandinavian peninsula in Europe

15. O(○)__ n: on the Arabian peninsula

16. P(○)__ u: on the Pacific coast of South America

17. Q __ __ __ r: on a peninsula near the Persian Gulf

18. R __ __ __ (○)__ a: in southeast Europe on the Black Sea

19. S __ (○)__ n: east of Portugal and south of France

20. T(○)__ __ __ y: in Asia Minor between the Mediterranean and Black Seas

21. U(○)__ __ __ a: in East Central Africa

22. V __ __ __ __ (○)__ (○)a: on the Caribbean coast of South America

23. W __ __ __ __ __ __ n S __ __ (○)a: in the South Pacific Ocean

24. Y __ (○)__ n: near Saudi Arabia on the Arabian Peninsula

25. Z __ __ __ e: south of Sudan and north of Angola in Central Africa

28. A STATELY FIND

Six states provide the answers in this exercise. If you correctly identify the state after one clue, score four points, after two clues, three points, and so on.

A. 1. Every odd-numbered letter in this six-letter state is a vowel. 2. It is bordered by an ocean and four other states. 3 Its state capital's letters can be rearranged to spell the word "males." 4. It is one of three states beginning with the 15th letter of the alphabet.

The state is _____ .

B. 1. This state contains the geographic center of the contiguous forty-eight states. 2. The six letters of this state form the last six letters of another state. 3. The movie *The Wizard of Oz* added to this state's fame. 4. Wild Bill Hickok, President Eisenhower, and aviatrix Amelia Earhart came from this state.

The state is _____ .

C. 1. This state is touched by eight other states. 2. This state whose name contains three sets of double letters is adjacent to another state whose name does the same. 3 The only vowel in this state's name is the letter *e*. 4. Knoxville, Memphis, and Nashville are cities in this state.

The state is _____ .

D. 1. Two Great Lakes are found in this state. 2. This state touches Canada. 3. The letters of its capital can be rearranged to spell ANY LAB. 4. Two U.S. presidents sharing the same last name were born in this state.

The state is _____ .

E. 1. Only one other state touches this state. 2. Its people are called Down Easters. 3. If you take away one letter from the name of its capital, you have spelled a month of the year. 4. Bowdoin College, located in this state, once had poet Henry Wadsworth Longfellow, future U.S. President Franklin Pierce, and novelist Nathaniel Hawthorne in attendance at the same time!

The state is _____ .

F. 1. Its entire eastern coast is water. 2. Its capital is the same name as one of our country's earliest presidents. 3. It has the Packers and Brewers. 4. Alphabetically, it's near the end of the list of states.

The state is _____ .

Name _____ Date _____ Period _____

29. COMPLETE THE COUNTRY

Each of the fifteen countries has had its first two and last two letters taken away. Luckily the list of countries has remained in its original alphabetical order to help you identify these countries. Fill in each country's missing letters. Then using the list of capitals below the last country, match the capitals with their correct countries by writing the letter in the space provided. The first one is done for you.

1. _D_   _AU_ STRAL _IA_

2. ___   __ __ LGI __ __

3. ___   __ __ AZ __ __

4. ___   __ __ NA __ __

5. ___   __ __ NMA __ __

6. ___   __ __ Y __ __

7. ___   __ __ EE __ __

8. ___   __ __ RA __ __

9. ___   __ __ XI __ __

10. ___   __ __ THERLAN __ __

11. ___   __ __ RW __ __

12. ___   __ __ KIST __ __

13. ___   __ __ RTUG __ __

14. ___   __ __ ITZERLA __ __

15. ___   __ __ NEZUE __ __

A. Cairo	F. Caracas	K. Brussels
B. Amsterdam	G. Oslo	L. Copenhagen
C. Brasilia	H. Bern	M. Jerusalem
D. Canberra	I. Athens	N. Lisbon
E. Islamabad	J. Ottawa	O. Mexico City

30. THERE'S ALWAYS A FIRST TIME

In the space provided write the letter corresponding to the correct date for the first time that each of these events occurred. If you have answered them all correctly, you will have spelled out the first big hit of a very famous singing group.

1. ____ Chewing gum was initially manufactured in (g) 1900 (h) 1655 (i) 1848 (j) 1798.

2. ____ London was the first city to exceed a population of 1,000,000 in (w) 1811 (x) 1570 (y) 1941 (z) 1329.

3. ____ The First World War began in (a) 1914 (b) 1687 (c) 1901 (d) 1599.

4. ____ The first appendix operation took place in (k) 1807 (l) 1772 (m) 1459 (n) 1887.

5. ____ The first public library started in England in (s) 1908 (t) 1608 (u) 1708 (v) 1808.

6. ____ The first postage stamp was issued in Paris in (t) 1653 (u) 1753 (v) 1853 (w) 1904.

7. ____ The first photograph of a living person was taken in (l) 1767 (m) 1500 (n) 1910 (o) 1838.

8. ____ America's first automobile parking meter was installed in Oklahoma City in (g) 1835 (h) 1935 (i) 1899 (j) 1765.

9. ____ The first fountain pen was made in Paris in (o) 1656 (p) 1756 (q) 1856 (r) 1902.

10. ____ Levi Strauss introduced the first pair of jeans in (j) 1650 (k) 1750 (l) 1850 (m) 1950.

11. ____ The first time an iron lung was used was in (a) 1808 (b) 1878 (c) 1908 (d) 1928.

12. ____ You could find the first magazine in Paris in (w) 1471 (x) 1572 (y) 1672 (z) 1772.

13. ____ The USA had its first automatic dishwasher in (m) 1569 (n) 1679 (o) 1889 (p) 1940.

14. ____ The first passenger elevator was installed in Paris in the year (t) 1643 (u) 1743 (v) 1843 (w) 1943.

15. ____ The first American policewoman began work in (r) 1910 (s) 1760 (t) 1955 (u) 1980.

16. ____ The first televised sporting event, a baseball game, was broadcast in (f) 1900 (g) 1899 (h) 1931 (i) 1949.

17. ____ Elizabeth Blackwell, the first woman doctor, worked in the year (a) 1849 (b) 1776 (c) 1668 (d) 1973.

18. ____ Mt. Holyoke, America's first women's college, opened in (m) 1737 (n) 1837 (o) 1937 (p) 1665.

19. ____ The plus and minus signs in math were initially used in (d) 1489 (e) 1238 (f) 1690 (g) 1900.

The song is _____.

Name _____ Date _____ Period _____

3I. LISTEN AND SPELL

Your teacher will dictate thirty sentences to you. In each sentence you will be asked to spell a specific word. Listen carefully to how the word is used within the sentence.

1. _____

2. _____

3. _____

4. _____

5. _____

6. _____

7. _____

8. _____

9. _____

10. _____

11. _____

12. _____

13. _____

14. _____

15. _____

16. _____

17. _____

18. _____

19. _____

20. _____

21. _____

22. _____

23. _____

24. _____

25. _____

26. _____

27. _____

28. _____

29. _____

30. _____

32. SPELLING FOR POINTS

Like the popular spelling crossword game Scrabble, this activity helps to improve spelling, vocabulary, and word recognition. Just as importantly, the competition is fun whether you do it individually or in groups. What a great combination!

Using the following point values for each letter, spell words of any length to see if you can construct the word with the highest point total.

A = 1	F = 4	K = 5	P = 3	U = 1	Z = 11
B = 3	G = 3	L = 2	Q = 11	V = 5	
C = 3	H = 4	M = 3	R = 1	W = 4	
D = 3	I = 1	N = 2	S = 1	X = 9	
E = 1	J = 9	O = 1	T = 1	Y = 5	

WORD   **POINT VALUE**

1. _____   _____
2. _____   _____
3. _____   _____
4. _____   _____
5. _____   _____
6. _____   _____
7. _____   _____
8. _____   _____
9. _____   _____
10. _____   _____

Name _____ Date _____ Period _____

33. SPELLING TOWARD 67

Here are twenty-five spelling words whose spellings can be confusing. If the word is correct, write *C* in the space. If the word is spelled incorrectly, spell it correctly. When you total the numbers of the words that are spelled correctly, you should have a total of 67. *(If the first three were misspelled, you would add 1 + 2 + 3.)*

1. _____ committment
2. _____ psycholegy
3. _____ sophomore
4. _____ medievel
5. _____ ninty
6. _____ cemetary
7. _____ rhythm
8. _____ goverment
9. _____ villian
10. _____ exstacy
11. _____ laboratory
12. _____ embarass
13. _____ temperment
14. _____ criticism
15. _____ excitable
16. _____ boundry
17. _____ accompany
18. _____ resistence
19. _____ prefered
20. _____ seperate
21. _____ shephard
22. _____ calender
23. _____ incidently
24. _____ violance
25. _____ absense

34. CHOOSING THE CORRECT SPELLING

Each number has three words next to it. Two of the three words are spelled incorrectly. Circle the letters of the words that are spelled correctly and record those letters in the spaces below the last set of words. If you've done that correctly, you'll find some familiar names there. Circle those familiar names.

1. j. acomplish   k. accumplish   l. accomplish
2. l. maneuver   m. manoover   n. maneuvar
3. a. eiligable   b. elligible   c. eligible
4. n. occurence   o. occurrence   p. occurrance
5. o. muscle   p. muscel   q. mustle
6. k. sherif   l. sheriff   m. sherriff
7. h. publisity   i. publicaty   j. publicity
8. d. grammer   e. grammar   f. gramar
9. l. receive   m. recieve   n. reseive
10. s. sallary   t. salary   u. salery
11. o. recommend   p. recomend   q. reccommend
12. m. boundery   n. boundary   o. boundry
13. g. existance   h. existence   i. existense
14. n. approvel   o. approval   p. approvil
15. o. among   p. amoung   q. ammong
16. s. alowance   t. allowance   u. allowence
17. i. analysis   j. analycis   k. anallysis
18. e. relevant   f. relevent   g. relivant
19. l. stratagy   m. strategy   n. stratigy
20. i. similar   j. similiar   k. simmilar
21. a. neice   b. niese   c. niece
22. f. foriegn   g. forreign   h. foreign
23. a. knowledge   b. knowlege   c. knowlidge
24. e. pronounce   f. pronounse   g. pronounnce
25. k. valluable   l. valuable   m. valueable

1	2	3	4	5	6	7	8	9	10	11	12	13

14	15	16	17	18	19	20	21	22	23	24	25

Name _____ Date _____ Period _____

35. WHERE THE LETTERS BELONG

Each of the fifteen words has one letter missing. From the string of letters below, select the letter that fills the space within each word. Unscramble the remaining letters to show a possible response to a joke.

a a a a a e e e e e e e e h h i i s t y

1. as__nine

2. critici__m

3. desir__ble

4. fr__ight

5. hindr__nce

6. inev__table

7. insur__nce

8. li__utenant

9. ph__sique

10. rep__tition

11. r__yme

12. s__rgeant

13. simil__r

14. strat__gy

15. venge__nce

The six remaining letters are: __ __ __ __ __ __

The answer to show a possible response to a joke is __ __ __ __ __ __ .

59

36. THE FORTY-FOUR HIDDEN NOUNS

Hidden within the sentences below are forty-four nouns—names of persons, places, things, or ideas. Circle the first letter of each noun and then record these letters, in order, in the spaces following the last sentence. If you've done this correctly, you will have spelled out a quote by Beatle John Lennon.

1. Luck is the instrument of one's foolishness.

2. Ellen showed much improvement since last summer.

3. On Wednesday we will show Howie our new automobile.

4. Toys can't replace hugs.

5. Another athlete will participate in the pentathlon instead of Paul.

6. Ecology and nature should be studied by students so that the world will be pre-served for humanity.

7. India is a land that depends on elephants more than Yugoslavia does.

8. Officials under the umbrella or their assistants near the rink can help you now.

9. An education in medicine has always been an asset.

10. The king had an interest in newspapers.

11. Several girls had the opportunity this Thursday to dye their hair.

12. The English enjoy their readings of Poe and Lawrence.

13. Usually his answers are refreshingly interesting.

14. The numbers and solutions can be easily located.

— — — — — — — — — — — — — — — —

— — — — — — — — — — — — — — — — —

— — — — — — — — — — .

Name _____ Date _____ Period _____

37. THESE THREE LETTERS ADD UP!

Each of the twenty-six letters of the alphabet has been assigned a point value to help you identify the twenty three-letter words whose definitions are given below. The total letter value of each word, including the letter given in each word, is in parentheses after the word. Using this grid, see how quickly you can spell the words.

Letter	A	B	C	D	E	F	G	H	I	J	K	L	M	N	O	P	Q	R	S	T
Value	1	2	3	4	5	6	7	8	9	10	11	12	13	14	15	16	17	18	19	20

Letter	U	V	W	X	Y	Z
Value	21	22	23	24	25	26

Example: a young child: __ O __ (55) The answer is *TOT* since each *T* is worth 20 and the *O* is worth 15 for a total of 55.

1. to talk much or idly: __ A __ (10)

2. an unruly crowd: __ __ B (30)

3. not cooked: __ A __ (42)

4. short-time fashion or style: __ A __ (11)

5. the lair of a wild animal: __ __ N (23)

6. an insect: __ N __ (35)

7. a one-digit number: __ I __ (52)

8. tint: __ __ E (34)

9. to throw slowly and in a high curve: __ O __ (29)

10. not forward: __ H __ (52)

11. a bony fish: __ E __ (22)

12. a box: __ I __ (25)

13. a Japanese coin: __ __ N (44)

14. to express pain: C __ __ (46)

15. a number of sheets for writing: __ A __ (21)

16. string used in tennis or fishing: __ E __ (39)

17. an animal doctor: __ E __ (47)

·18. to disturb or annoy: __ __ X (51)

19. a small bit: N __ __ (39)

20. part of a circle: __ R __ (22)

38. VOCABULARY PUZZLER

Please write the relationship next to each pair of words. In the space provided, write whether the two words are synonyms (*S*) or opposites (*O*).

1. ____ jovial: unhappy

2. ____ soothing: painful

3. ____ vigor: lassitude

4. ____ trivial: important

5. ____ vulnerable: unprotected

6. ____ essential: extraneous

7. ____ detrimental: beneficial

8. ____ prosperous: indigent

9. ____ somber: gloomy

10. ____ terse: succinct

11. ____ opacity: clarity

12. ____ reprove: applaud

13. ____ prolong: shorten

14. ____ viable: unworkable

15. ____ enlighten: confuse

16. ____ inquisitive: curious

17. ____ solitary: gregarious

18. ____ modest: extreme

19. ____ progressive: regressive

20. ____ plausible: believable

21. ____ serene: tranquil

22. ____ exotic: common

23. ____ ruffle: smooth

24. ____ capricious: unpredictable

25. ____ sparing: economical

39. ANOTHER VOCABULARY PUZZLER

In the space provided, write whether the two words are synonyms (*S*) or opposites (*O*).

1. ____ verify: disprove

2. ____ flourish: wither

3. ____ incidental: important

4. ____ morose: gleeful

5. ____ rotund: gaunt

6. ____ widespread: contained

7. ____ expunge: erase

8. ____ repulse: reject

9. ____ rare: usual

10. ____ meticulous: careless

11. ____ effectual: ineffective

12. ____ reserved: immodest

13. ____ thrash: embrace

14. ____ harmony: discord

15. ____ inspire: discourage

16. ____ muster: disperse

17. ____ integrity: dishonesty

18. ____ wary: cautious

19. ____ gigantic: miniscule

20. ____ barren: fertile

21. ____ corrupt: pure

22. ____ devotion: disloyalty

23. ____ obfuscate: clarify

24. ____ vivid: dim

25. ____ surfeit: excess

40. MATCHING THEM UP

Match each of these words, listed alphabetically from left to right, with its synonym. Each word is used only once.

antiquated   durable   enhance   ethical   inhibit
malice   optimism   raucous   restrict   scale
severe   spurious   stolid   stupor   submissive
swagger   trite   uproar   vague   zany

1. _____ to strut

2. _____ confusion

3. _____ ill-will

4. _____ fake

5. _____ with no emotion

6. _____ to limit

7. _____ positive outlook

8. _____ strict

9. _____ to restrain

10. _____ crazy

11. _____ not defiant

12. _____ moral

13. _____ to improve

14. _____ able to withstand

15. _____ rough-sounding

16. _____ unclear

17. _____ mental dullness

18. _____ old

19. _____ to climb up

20. _____ stale

Name _____ Date _____ Period _____

41. THE LETTER A

The answers to the following questions all begin with the letter *A*. Write your answers in the spaces provided.

1. _____ defensive or protective covering

2. _____ the bar connecting two opposite wheels on an automobile

3. _____ the air surrounding the earth

4. _____ an excuse used to avoid punishment

5. _____ word used at the end of a prayer

6. _____ highly skilled

7. _____ fuss or trouble

8. _____ hypersensitivity to a particular substance

9. _____ opinion given as to what to do

10. _____ a playing card

11. _____ to use wrongly or to mistreat

12. _____ a man who heads a monastery

13. _____ to gain by one's own efforts

14. _____ large South American river

15. _____ Greek philosopher

16. _____ U.S. state whose capital is Little Rock

17. _____ another name for Veterans Day

18. _____ legendary sunken country in the Atlantic

19. _____ island continent between the South Pacific and Indian Oceans

20. _____ group of Portuguese islands

65

42. POTPOURRI GUESS ME IN THREE CLUES GAME

Your teacher will read a series of clues concerning ten famous people. Select particular words or phrases that help you to identify each person. Record the clues, answers, and points in the spaces provided.

1. _____ _____ _____
   Answer: _____ Points: _____

2. _____ _____ _____
   Answer: _____ Points: _____

3. _____ _____ _____
   Answer: _____ Points: _____

4. _____ _____ _____
   Answer: _____ Points: _____

5. _____ _____ _____
   Answer: _____ Points: _____

6. _____ _____ _____
   Answer: _____ Points: _____

7. _____ _____ _____
   Answer: _____ Points: _____

8. _____ _____ _____
   Answer: _____ Points: _____

9. _____ _____ _____
   Answer: _____ Points: _____

10. _____ _____ _____
    Answer: _____ Points: _____

The total number of points accumulated is _____ .

43. ENGLISH CLASS GUESS WHICH AUTHOR I AM GAME

Your teacher will read a series of clues concerning ten famous authors. Select particular words or phrases that help you to identify each person. Record the clues, answers, and points in the spaces provided.

1. _____ _____ _____

   Answer: _____ Points: _____

2. _____ _____ _____

   Answer: _____ Points: _____

3. _____ _____ _____

   Answer: _____ Points: _____

4. _____ _____ _____

   Answer: _____ Points: _____

5. _____ _____ _____

   Answer: _____ Points: _____

6. _____ _____ _____

   Answer: _____ Points: _____

7. _____ _____ _____

   Answer: _____ Points: _____

8. _____ _____ _____

   Answer: _____ Points: _____

9. _____ _____ _____

   Answer: _____ Points: _____

10. _____ _____ _____

   Answer: _____ Points: _____

The total number of points accumulated is _____ .

Name _____ Date _____ Period _____

44. LITERATURE AND AUTHORS (PART ONE)

Start to accumulate points by correctly answering these questions dealing with literature and authors. The category is listed above the group of questions, and the point value of each question is found within parentheses before the question's number. Write your answers in the spaces provided. Total up your points to see how you did. Good luck!

MARK TWAIN

(10) 1. He was born in the city of Florida in this state. _____

(20) 2. She was Tom Sawyer's girlfriend. _____

(30) 3. Twain's notes regarding his travels through Europe are compiled in this book. _____

(40) 4. Twain is buried in this state. _____

(50) 5. His birth and death coincided with this scientific event. _____

Total points: _____

AMERICAN AUTHORS

(10) 1. His real name was Theodor Geisel. _____

(20) 2. In 1836 he married his cousin, Virginia Clemm, a thirteen year old. _____

(30) 3. His *Grapes of Wrath* featured the Joad family. _____

(40) 4. Her father, a philosopher, teacher, and poet, was superintendent of the Concord, Massachusetts, schools. _____

(50) 5. A Harvard graduate, he wrote *The Witches of Eastwick* which was later made into a feature film. _____

Total points: _____

AMERICAN PLAYWRIGHTS

(10) 1. His plays include *Barefoot in the Park* and *The Odd Couple*. _____

(20) 2. William Gibson's *The Miracle Worker* is the story of Annie Sullivan and this young lady, her most famous student. _____

(30) 3. I wrote *Murder in the Cathedral*, *The Cocktail Party*, and *Family Reunion*. _____

(40) 4. I was once married to Marilyn Monroe. _____

(50) 5. This was Thornton Wilder's play that was later made into the musical *Hello Dolly*. _____

Total points: _____

Name _____ Date _____ Period _____

45. LITERATURE AND AUTHORS (PART TWO)

Accumulate points as you display your knowledge of literature and authors. The category is listed above the group of questions, and the point value of each question is found within parentheses before the question's number. Write your answers in the spaces provided. Total your points to see how well you did. Good luck!

AMERICAN POETS

(10) 1. "Nevermore" will you forget his raven. _____

(20) 2. He recited his poetry at the inauguration of President John Fitzgerald Kennedy in 1961. _____

(30) 3. His poem, "Harlem," asks, "What happens to a dream deferred?" _____

(40) 4. Lucinda Matlock was one of his Spoon River residents.

(50) 5. Emily Dickinson told us that because she could not stop for this, it gladly stopped for her. _____

Total points: _____

BLACK WRITERS

(10) 1. His *Roots* became a smash television miniseries. _____

(20) 2. My novel, *Go Tell It on the Mountain*, centers around race relations. _____

(30) 3. *Song of Solomon* earned her a Pulitzer prize. _____

(40) 4. This *Invisible Man* author made his mark with this American classic. _____

(50) 5. She entitled her work *To Be Young, Gifted and Black*. _____

Total points: _____

AMERICAN AUTHORS

(10) 1. His 1925 novel, *The Great Gatsby*, is read by many high-school students. _____

(20) 2. She was known as the Belle of Amherst. _____

(30) 3. His works are set in Yoknapatawpha County, Mississippi. _____

(40) 4. His memoirs of Paris were published in book form entitled *A Moveable Feast*. _____

(50) 5. She popularized the term "a lost generation" to describe the people who came to maturity between World War I and the Great Depression. _____

Total points: _____

46. THE SCIENCE GUESS WHO AM I GAME

Your teacher will read a series of clues concerning ten famous scientists. Select particular words or phrases that help you to identify each person. Record the clues, answers, and points in the spaces provided.

1. _____ _____ _____
   Answer: _____ Points: _____

2. _____ _____ _____
   Answer: _____ Points: _____

3. _____ _____ _____
   Answer: _____ Points: _____

4. _____ _____ _____
   Answer: _____ Points: _____

5. _____ _____ _____
   Answer: _____ Points: _____

6. _____ _____ _____
   Answer: _____ Points: _____

7. _____ _____ _____
   Answer: _____ Points: _____

8. _____ _____ _____
   Answer: _____ Points: _____

9. _____ _____ _____
   Answer: _____ Points: _____

10. _____ _____ _____
    Answer: _____ Points: _____

The total number of points accumulated is _____ .

47. SCIENTIFIC QUESTIONS

Science is incredible. The numbers in this activity deal with the numbers of some incredible scientific statistics. See how well you know your science numbers by matching up the correct questions in Group One with the correct numbers in Group Two. The answers contain the names of two boys and one girl.

GROUP ONE

A. What is the number of miles per hour that a raindrop falls?

B. What is the average number of days that the South Pole has no sunlight each year?

C. What is the speed of light in miles per second?

D. How long is the Nile River, the world's longest river?

E. How deep is Lake Baikal, the deepest lake in the world?

F. What is the temperature of the sun's center in degrees Fahrenheit?

G. What percent of days is it sunny in Yuma, Arizona?

H. What percent of the Earth's surface is land?

I. What is the number of hours it takes a human being to fully digest his food?

J. How many years old is the sun?

K. What is the average depth of the ocean's floor?

L. What is a human being's average number of eye blinks per day?

M. How many miles long is the Grand Canyon?

N. How high is Mt. McKinley, the highest point in the United States?

O. What is the Earth's circumference (in miles) at the equator?

GROUP TWO

1. _____ 186,000	6. _____ 20,320 feet	11. _____ 90
2. _____ 27,000,000	7. _____ 13,124 feet	12. _____ 7
3. _____ 4.5 billion	8. _____ 5,314	13. _____ 15
4. _____ 24,902	9. _____ 4,145	14. _____ 17,000
5. _____ 30	10. _____ 217	15. _____ 182

48. WHICH SCIENCE????

Here is an opportunity to classify forty words under their proper headings. Next to each term write the Letters *ES* if it is primarily found in the science of Earth science, *B* if it's in biology, *C* if it's in chemistry, and *P* if it's in physics.

1. _____ atomic number

2. _____ kinetic energy

3. _____ fibula

4. _____ fault

5. _____ galvanometer

6. _____ endocrine

7. _____ ohm

8. _____ tectonics

9. _____ superconductor

10. _____ electron

11. _____ reproductive

12. _____ dunes

13. _____ thermodynamics

14. _____ ampere

15. _____ weathering

16. _____ periodic table

17. _____ Fahrenheit scale

18. _____ paleontologist

19. _____ voltage

20. _____ circulatory system

21. _____ ion

22. _____ exfoliation

23. _____ joule

24. _____ digestive

25. _____ chlorofluorocarbons

26. _____ nutrition

27. _____ lava

28. _____ fulcrum

29. _____ Boyle's Law

30. _____ hertz

31. _____ continental drift

32. _____ fertilization

33. _____ valence

34. _____ sedimentary rocks

35. _____ humerus

36. _____ corrosion

37. _____ big bang theory

38. _____ fibia

39. _____ slag

40. _____ quantum numbers

Name _____ Date _____ Period _____

49. THE TERMS OF SCIENCE

Here are fourteen terms from various sciences. If you have matched the terms correctly, each group should have the same numerical total. An *A* answer is worth 1, a *B* is worth 2, a *C* is worth 3, and a *D* is worth 4. Circle the letter and write its numerical value in the space provided. The first one is done for you.

GROUP ONE

1. __3__ The smallest part of an element is the (A) core (B) neutron (C) atom (D) electron.

2. _____ The outer layer of the Earth's surface is called the (A) rock (B) slag (C) plate (D) crust.

3. _____ The amount of space occupied by matter is called the (A) volume (B) area (C) weight (D) mixture.

4. _____ A group of atoms that share electrons is a (A) molecule (B) joint (C) proton (D) spur.

5. _____ In the Celsius scale water boils at (A) 212 degrees (B) 100 degrees (C) 98.6 degrees (D) 238 degrees.

6. _____ The temperature at which water vapor condenses to a liquid is known as (A) vaporization (B) dew point (C) neither A nor B (D) both A and B.

7. _____ Tides are caused by the gravitational attraction of the (A) sun (B) meteors (C) moon (D) none of these.

TOTAL: _____

GROUP TWO

8. _____ The process by which water changes from a liquid to a gas is called (A) evaporation (B) condensation (C) dew process (D) convection.

9. _____ A front, the area of contact between two air masses of different temperatures, is a term used primarily in which science? (A) biology (B) meteorology (C) chemistry (D) physics.

10. _____ The most recently coined term of the four terms that follow is (A) weather forecast (B) smog (C) tides (D) Fahrenheit scale.

11. _____ The imaginary line about which an object spins is called the (A) circumference (B) radius (C) lever (D) axis.

12. _____ How many planets constitute the outer planets? (A) six (B) eight (C) five (D) three.

13. _____ Another term for a meteor is (A) shooting star (B) spectacle (C) asteroid (D) nebula.

14. _____ How many cubic centimeters are in a liter? (A) 10 (B) 100 (C) 1,000 (D) 10,000.

TOTAL: _____

73

Name _____ Date _____ Period _____

50. FADED SCIENCE HEADLINES

A stack of newspapers whose headlines contain important advances in science has been found in a dusty attic. The problem is that the sun has faded a number of these headlines. The dates are given, but you must fill in the faded information. Write the missing words in their proper spaces.

1. 1543 Nicolaus _____ says planets circle around the _____.

2. 1628 William _____ demonstrates the circulation of blood.

3. 1642 Blaise _____ constructs the first adding machine to perform the operation of carrying.

4. 1666 Sir _____ _____ reflects on the fall of an apple and ponders universal gravitation.

5. 1798 Edward _____ finds a _____ against smallpox.

6. 1834 Cyrus _____ patents the cotton _____.

7. 1859 Charles _____ publishes his book entitled *Origin of* _____.

8. 1865 Louis _____ finds way to destroy _____ with heat.

9. 1867 Alfred Nobel manufactures _____ for blasting purposes.

10. 1876 Alexander _____ _____ patents the _____.

11. 1879 Ivan _____ works on the conditioned _____ theory.

12. 1892 Rudolf _____ patents his heavy oil engine.

13. 1895 Guglielmo _____ invents the wireless _____.

14. 1905 Albert _____ announces his theory of _____.

15. 1942 Enrico _____ and friends build the first self-sustaining _____ reactor.

51. SCIENTIFIC THINGS TO THINK ABOUT

Here are seven scientific questions that raise some interesting discussion topics. In the space provided, write the reason each of these actions occurs. Compare your responses with those of your classmates.

1. Are humans today smarter than humans of 10,000 years ago?

2. What natural elements can take credit for the formation of the Grand Canyon?

3. Why do horses used for pulling wagons wear blinders?

4. Why is the Tower of Pisa leaning? What reason within the Tower itself could cause its collapse?

5. How does a submarine operate?

6. Who tend to develop more wrinkles as they age—men or women? Why?

7. Why is red used for stop signs, danger signals, and brake lights?

(Used with permission from *Science Is: A Source Book of Fascinating Facts, Projects and Activities*, by Susan V. Bosak. 1992. New York, NY: Scholastic, 1-800-325-6149.)

Section Three

LANGUAGE AND WRITING

52. WHEN THE ACTION FITS THE MOOD

Here are fifteen common actions. When would you chuckle? grimace? beam? Here is your chance to show your vocabulary prowess. In the space provided, give the meaning of the word **or** give an example of when this action is appropriate. Compare your answers with those of your classmates.

1. beam _____

2. chuckle _____

3. enchant _____

4. flinch _____

5. frown _____

6. giggle _____

7. glare _____

8. gloat _____

9. goad _____

10. grimace _____

11. grunt _____

12. guffaw _____

13. howl _____

14. leer _____

15. malign _____

Name _____ Date _____ Period _____

53. MORE ACTIONS THAT FIT THE MOOD

These fifteen words are actions that we do quite often. Surely you have pondered over something that is important to you or scowled about an event or action that unfortunately took place. In the space provided, write either the word's meaning **or** an occasion when the word is appropriate to the mood.

1. ponder _____

2. prate _____

3. quail _____

4. quaver _____

5. rail _____

6. resent _____

7. scoff _____

8. scowl _____

9. smirk _____

10. snarl _____

11. sneer _____

12. stew _____

13. subdue _____

14. wince _____

15. yelp _____

54. REARRANGING WORDS

Here are twenty-five words that can be rearranged to form another word. You will not have to add or delete any letters. And you'll need to do is rearrange the letters that are already there. Write the newly formed word in the space provided. The first one is done for you.

1. __laced__   decal
2. _____   wrong
3. _____   baser
4. _____   recoated
5. _____   lived
6. _____   tracer
7. _____   lemon
8. _____   burnt
9. _____   thorn
10. _____   lance
11. _____   drawer
12. _____   waste
13. _____   march
14. _____   knits
15. _____   wrest
16. _____   tablet
17. _____   strop
18. _____   least
19. _____   flesh
20. _____   demand
21. _____   cheap
22. _____   strut
23. _____   clasp
24. _____   table
25. _____   teach

55. HOW A DEED BECOMES A STAR

In only four steps, changing only one letter at a time, the word "deed" can become the word "star." The progression goes like this: Starting with "deed," the word changes to "dee**r**," then to "de**a**r," then to "**s**ear," and, finally, to "s**t**ar." Here are ten words with the starting word and the word that it will, four steps later, become. Write the progression in the spaces provided.

1. Change bath to mole.

_____

2. Change save to bond.

_____

3. Change coat to meld.

_____

4. Change flax to prey.

_____

5. Change clay to boot.

_____

6. Change wind to sage.

_____

7. Change fame to tilt.

_____

8. Change sure to font.

_____

9. Change bank to lord.

_____

10. Change grip to team.

_____

56. WHAT IF THERE WERE NO VOWELS?

Vowels don't exist here. Identify these quotations by writing the full quotation, including vowels, beneath each quote. When finished, discuss the quotations with your classmates.

1. H wh hstts s lst.

_____

2. Ths r th tms tht tr mn's sls.

_____

3. Clnlnss s nxt t gdlnss.

_____

4. pnny svd s pnny rnd.

_____

5. Whn th ct's wy, th mc wll ply.

_____

6. n ppl dy kps th dctr wy.

_____

7. Th wsst mn fllw thr wn drctns.

_____

8. vry cld hs slvr lnng.

_____

9. Cnscnc mks cwrds f s ll.

_____

10. Knwldg s pwr.

_____

11. Brvty s th sl f wt.

_____

12. t s sy t dsps wht y cnnt gt.

_____

57. THE DOUBLE LETTERS OF FOODS

The names of many of the foods we eat contain double letters. Apples and beets are two examples. In the spaces below, name as many foods containing double letters as you can. Finding ten names is good, fifteen makes you a future chef, and twenty gives you a possible occupation as a food connoisseur. No specific brand names are allowed.

1. _____
2. _____
3. _____
4. _____
5. _____
6. _____
7. _____
8. _____
9. _____
10. _____

11. _____
12. _____
13. _____
14. _____
15. _____
16. _____
17. _____
18. _____
19. _____
20. _____

Bonus: Name two drinks that have double letters in them.

_____ and _____

Name _____   Date _____   Period _____

58. LET'S ELIMINATE WAR AND HATE

War and hate are out in this exercise! The letters *w-a-r* (always in order, though not necessarily consecutively) have been removed from each of the words in column A, with any resulting spaces closed up. The same holds true for column B where the letters *h-a-t-e* have been eliminated. The first ones are already done for you.

COLUMN A

1. tod   <u>toward</u>
2. t   _____
3. red   _____
4. se   _____
5. cod   _____
6. bee   _____
7. hf   _____
8. homed   _____
9. ad   _____
10. sete   _____
11. rior   _____
12. eer   _____
13. ind   _____
14. sm   _____
15. den   _____

COLUMN B

1. ed   <u>heated</u>
2. str   _____
3. ern   _____
4. esit   _____
5. cs   _____
6. exusd   _____
7. posph   _____
8. wver   _____
9. reabilit   _____
10. ctr   _____
11. cpr   _____
12. aspyxi   _____
13. encnd   _____
14. anniil   _____
15. sn   _____

59. THE ART OF DECODING

Use the code below to decode each of these sentences, mottoes, or phrases. To make it interesting, we have purposely left out some of the numbers in the sentences.

<u>G</u> <u>O</u> <u>O</u> <u>D</u> <u>L</u> <u>U</u> <u>C</u> <u>K</u>!
7 15 15 4   12 21 3 11

A=1 B=2 C=3 D=4 E=5 F=6 G=7 H=8 I=9 J=10 K=11 L=12 M=13 N=14 O=15 P=16 Q=17
R=18 S=19 T=20 U=21 V=22 W=23 X=24 Y=25 Z=26

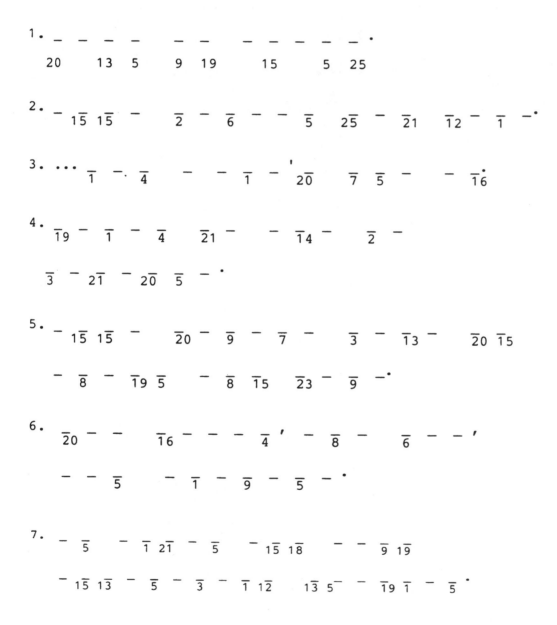

1. _ _ _ _   _ _   _ _ _ _ .
   20 13 5 9 19 15 5 25

2. _ __ __ _   _ _ _ _   _ _ __ __ _ __ __ _ __ _ .
     15 15   2   6   5 25   21 12   1

3. ... __ _ __   _ _ __ _ '_ __ __ _   _ __ .
       1   4   1   20 7 5   16

4. __ _ __ __ _   _ __ _ __ _
   19 1 4 21   14   2

   __ _ __ _ __ _ _ .
   3   21   20 5

5. _ __ __ _   __ _ __ _ __ _   __ _ __ _   __ __
     15 15   20 9   7   3   13   20 15

   _ __ _   __ __ _   _ __ __ __ _ __ .
     8   19 5   8 15 23   9

6. __ _ _   __ _ _ _ __ '_ __ _   __ _ _ '
   20   16   4   8   6

   _ _ __ _   _ __ _ __ _ __ _ .
      5   1   9   5

7. _ __ _   __ __ _ __ _   __ __ _   _ __ __
      5   1 21   5   15 18   9 19

   _ __ __ _   __ _ __ _ __ _ __ __ _ __ __ _ __ __ _ .
    15 13   5   3   1 12   13 5   19 1   5

60. HAVE A HEART

Many of our everyday expressions include a reference to body parts. In the spaces provided, write what each of these expressions means.

1. have a heart _____

2. keep an eye on him _____

3. in the palm of your hand _____

4. tongue-tied _____

5. heart breaker _____

6. know it by heart _____

7. use elbow grease _____

8. an eyesore _____

9. eye-catcher _____

10. see eye to eye _____

11. an eye for an eye _____

12. catch one's eye _____

13. give him the eye _____

14. in the public eye _____

15. make eyes at _____

16. change of heart _____

17. eat one's heart out _____

18. one's heart is in the right place _____

19. steal his heart _____

20. from the bottom of my heart _____

87

61. AN OUT OF BODY EXPERIENCE

Fifteen words better known as body parts are the answers to this exercise. Here they are used in a different context. Write the words in the correct spaces. Each word is used only once.

back	hand	mouth
ear	head	neck
elbow	heel	nose
eye	leg	shoulder
foot	lip	tongue

1. Please hand me that _____ of corn.

2. You selected a nice _____ of bananas.

3. The _____ of lettuce did not look tasty.

4. The boaters were nearing the _____ of the river.

5. His toes could feel sand near the _____ of the bed.

6. The meteorologist explained about the _____ of the storm.

7. There was some dust on the _____ of the drinking glass.

8. What is the measurement of that _____ of the triangle?

9. The man who stole money from the elderly was described as a(n) _____ in the newspaper.

10. He slapped the criminal with the _____ of his hand.

11. We found the blockage at the pipe's _____.

12. The captain directed the _____ of the ship into the narrow opening by the pier.

13. Unfortunately, I cracked the _____ of the violin.

14. If in trouble, pull the car off onto the _____ of the road.

15. The lace was caught under the shoe's _____.

62. TRIPLE PLAY

The word "rest" means all three of these: to relax, a musical term, and the remainder. In each exercise below, one word fits the definitions of the three words or terms in the group. Write the correct word in the space provided.

1. _____ portion of cabbage, chief of state, to lead

2. _____ length measurement, body part, the end of a bed

3. _____ tennis term, matching collection of silverware, number of couples needed for a square dance

4. _____ ruler, checkers' piece, playing card

5. _____ girl's name, retort, a sudden rushing forth

6. _____ military unit, guests, habitual associates

7. _____ the pulp of a tooth, emotional control, cord-like fiber in the human body

8. _____ sudden fall of a business, a loud, sudden noise, a breaking into pieces

9. _____ a duck's sound, charlatan, an untrained person who practices medicine

10. _____ work, to move slowly and without difficulty, period of childbirth

11. _____ to get a monopoly on, secluded place, place where surfaces meet to form an angle

12. _____ thin piece of metal, a dish, part of a denture

13. _____ to move in water, to beat, a table tennis necessity

14. _____ beverage container, golfing container, bowl portion of a drinking vessel

15. _____ a sporting contest, birds or animals hunted for sport, recreation

16. _____ soft feathers, football term, in a bad condition

17. _____ to feel hot, to consume as fuel, to set on fire

18. _____ to endure, final, farthest from the first

19. _____ to move by hopping lightly, a boy's name, to pass over

20. _____ a boy's name, to throw quickly, a cut of beef

Name _____ Date _____ Period _____

63. A TRIP TO THE RESTAURANT

The menu in this restaurant is a bit different. The owners, former English and science teachers, believe in making the customers work for their food. Thus, instead of simply listing the foods, the owners define each part of the menu. The foods are listed alphabetically with **beans** as the first food. Meats, seafood, fruits, vegetables, and drinks are included on this menu. Write your answers in the appropriate spaces.

1. ____beans____ products of a leguminous plant of the species of a genus of the pea family

2. _____ made from grain, especially malted barley, fermented by yeast and flavored with hops

3. _____ the fleshy, orange-red roots of the cultivated strain of plant of the *umbel* family

4. _____ the flesh of the gallinaceous farm bird

5. _____ the soft, edible parts of an edible, hard-shelled bivalve mollusk

6. _____ dark-brown aromatic drink made by brewing in water the roasted and ground beanlike seeds of a tall tropical shrub

7. _____ a cultivated American cereal plant of the grass family

8. _____ long fruits, with a green rind and firm, white flesh, gathered before fully mature

9. _____ the leaves of a hardy, annual composite plant

10. _____ the product of a lactating mature female member of domestic cattle

11. _____ the starchy, brown-skinned or red-skinned tubers of a widely cultivated plant of the nightshade family

12. _____ the starchy seeds or grains of an aquatic cereal grass grown especially in the Orient

13. _____ small, slender, long-tailed decapod marine creature

14. _____ a slice of meat, especially beef, cut thick for frying

64. A PAGE OF TOM SWIFTIES

Edward Stratemeyer created the character, Tom Swift. In his books about Tom Swift and Tom's companions, Stratemeyer often used adverbs to describe various actions. Thus, words such as wisely, quickly, or innocently were common in Stratemeyer's books. Today a sentence such as, "'The kittens are beautiful," said Tom *literally,* is called a Tom Swiftie since kittens and literally (a litter of kittens) are a play on words. Match the sentences with the adverbs that correctly complete the Tom Swifties.

1. ____ "I want to get the ten pin," the bowler said _____.
2. ____ "I'd like to land on the prairie," the pilot said _____.
3. ____ "I'll need more gas," the anesthesiologist said _____.
4. ____ "Please be quiet in this study room," the librarian said _____.
5. ____ "I'll answer that," the debater said _____.
6. ____ "Please hand me the brushes," the painter said _____.
7. ____ "I could use more sugar," the baker said _____.
8. ____ "Anything I can do for you, boss?" the assistant asked _____.
9. ____ "I can do it myself," the electrician responded _____.
10. ____ "I'll help all the people in our parish," the priest said _____.
11. ____ "You will need to see me again very soon," the chiropractor said

   _____.

12. ____ "I don't need your snide remarks," the battery salesman answered

   _____.

13. ____ "I will find that missing student soon," the attendance officer said

   _____.

14. ____ "This is the best play I've ever seen," the drama critic remarked

   _____.

15. ____ "We don't need any more war," the peace marchers chanted _____.

a. absent-mindedly
b. affirmatively
c. bookishly
d. caustically
e. colorfully
f. disarmingly
g. disjointedly
h. helpfully
i. painlessly
j. plainly
k. religiously
l. shortly
m. sparingly
n. sweetly
o. theatrically

65. ANOTHER PAGE OF TOM SWIFTIES

Here are some more Tom Swifties. Write the letter of the correct adverb in the space provided.

1. ____ "I'll need to replace that cracked window," the salesman said _____.

2. ____ "The ball will be thrown right to you," the quarterback said _____.

3. ____ "I can't meet with you now," the denture maker said _____.

4. ____ "You will look just gorgeous," the hairdresser said _____.

5. ____ "You'll be on your feet in no time," the cardiologist told the patient _____.

6. ____ "I will lose fifteen pounds in a few weeks," the dieter said _____.

7. ____ "You don't want to read the Richter scale," the seismologist said _____.

8. ____ "Here comes one right down the middle," the pitcher said _____.

9. ____ "I will grace your magazine's cover," the model said _____.

10. ____ "We'll never play this piece correctly," the musical conductor complained _____.

11. ____ "I can never do it as bravely as you," the coward said _____.

12. ____ "You will devise your own theory," the philosopher said _____.

13. ____ "I'll call the doctor for you," the nurse said _____.

14. ____ "We can't fit any more garbage in this truck," the driver said _____.

15. ____ "I found some more liquid detergent," the boy said _____.

a. beautifully
b. disconcertedly
c. discouragingly
d. falsely
e. heartily
f. hospitably
g. joyfully
h. painfully
i. passingly
j. shakingly
k. strikingly
l. teasingly
m. thoughtfully
n. trimly
o. wastefully

66. FIRST NAMES HIDDEN IN THE SENTENCES

Fifteen boys' and girls' first names have been hidden within these sentences. Underline the names in each sentence. The first one is done for you.

1. The lunch advertisements were very interesting.

2. I can't convince her to go if she doesn't want to.

3. He likes to yell entirely too much if you ask me.

4. For the last event of the night, we would like you to lead us.

5. We are now featuring an entire new line of clothing.

6. Please bring in the flock at eleven o'clock for water.

7. He's merry and sweet, according to his teachers at preschool.

8. The coat will need a few alterations.

9. Please write your name down on the archery list.

10. The animals we will report on are the cat, hyena, elephant, and dog.

11. Can one gram be registered with the authorities?

12. In Alaska, rental homes are priced much cheaper than previously.

13. The American flag has colors of red, white, and blue.

14. Her garden is everything to her.

15. When leaving, we never leave our doors unlocked.

67. COMPLETING THE PARAGRAPH USING STRONG VOCABULARY WORDS

Ten vocabulary words will complete this paragraph. Please fill in each word in its proper space. Each word is used only once.

diminish   rebuffed   sullen   tardy   valid

pompous   sluggish   surmised   tirade   wooden

When the high school student who constantly overslept was again marked

(1) _____ to school, the normally expressionless, (2) _____-faced

assistant principal launched into a (3) _____ about the (4) _____

teenager's bad habits. The sixteen-year-old acknowledged that the principal had a

(5) _____ complaint. Trying to (6) _____ the severity of the punish-

ment, the student (7) _____ that if he tried to humor the (8) _____

administrator, who thought so highly of himself, punishment might not be in the stu-

dent's future. When the principal (9) _____ all the boy's pleas, the student

became quite (10) _____ and slowly left the room crying.

Name _____ Date _____ Period _____

68. COMPLETING SOME SENTENCES

Each of these ten words is used once. Fill in the most appropriate word to complete the sentence's idea. There is no need to change the word's form.

kindled	ominous	sporadic	synchronize	variable
monarch	ratify	stalemate	tranquil	vociferous

1. The _____ clouds warned us of the impending storm.

2. We must _____ our watches so that all the runners will be timed properly.

3. It was necessary for both sides to _____ the contract before releasing the news to the press.

4. Since the student's efforts were _____, his grades were equally inconsistent.

5. The reigning _____ was quite popular in England.

6. Negotiations reached a _____ when both sides refused to sit at the bargaining table any longer.

7. There is no more peaceful sight than the _____ pond at sunset.

8. The _____ crowd showed their anger and resentment at the school board meeting.

9. _____ weather conditions must not be taken lightly when people set out on a journey across the wide lake.

10. The patient's improved condition _____ hope in the heart of the dedicated doctor.

Name _____ Date _____ Period _____

69. RUNNING THE ALPHABET

When a billiards player uninterruptedly knocks every ball into a pocket, he has "run the table." Though you won't play billiards here, you will still have the opportunity to run, but you will "run the alphabet." In column A list <u>verbs</u> beginning with the letter in the left hand margin. In column B do the same for <u>adjectives</u> and in column C do the same for <u>adverbs</u>. Each word must be at least five letters and no word form can be used twice. Give yourself one point for each correct answer. The letter <u>a</u> is already done for you.

COLUMN A	COLUMN B	COLUMN C
a. argue	awful	astutely
b.		
c.		
d.		
e.		
f.		
g.		
h.		
i.		
j.		
k.		
l.		
m.		
n.		
o.		
p.		
q.		
r.		
s.		
t.		
u.		
v.		
w.		
x.		
y.		
z.		

Copyright © 1996 by John Wiley & Sons, Inc.

Name _____ Date _____ Period _____

70. MRS. MALAPROP HAS ARRIVED

Mrs. Malaprop, a character in Richard Brinsley Sheridan's play, *The Rivals*, had a knack for making ludicrous blunders in her use of words. An example of a malapropism is "Too many cooks spoil the cloth." Of course, the correct proverb is "Too many cooks spoil the broth." Correct these malapropisms by writing the correct word in the space provided. The word that needs to be corrected is underlined. The first one is done for you. Be prepared to explain the meanings of these proverbs and expressions.

1. She is a wolf in <u>sheik</u>'s clothing. <u>sheep's</u>

2. Don't put all your <u>pegs</u> in one basket. _____

3. After the embarrassing incident he had <u>mustard</u> on his face. _____

4. You can lead a horse to water, but you can't make it <u>sink</u>. _____

5. <u>Animosity</u> killed the cat. _____

6. Birds of a <u>weather</u> flock together. _____

7. Don't count your <u>eggs</u> before they hatch. _____

8. I was between a rock and a <u>hot</u> plate. _____

9. You are the apple of my <u>pie</u>. _____

10. It's time to pay the <u>wiper</u>. _____

11. He wanted to steal another's <u>blunder</u>. _____

12. Tim was caught <u>dead</u>-handed by the police. _____

13. Yvonne wanted to take the bull by the <u>corns</u>. _____

14. Wally didn't want to <u>chill</u> the beans. _____

Name _____ Date _____ Period _____

71. READING IN A WHOLE NEW WAY

RUYS? S,UR! Until you get the hang of it, these sentences may appear quite cryptic. They say, "Are you wise? Yes, you are!" Using your brains, ears, and imagination, write the words that comprise these sentences. Stick with them and have some fun!

1. URAQT,LN _____

2. UREZ2TS _____

3. RUOK? _____

4. URXLN! _____

5. URKTSNME _____

6. NGNDDR2BUTS _____

7. ILW _____

8. YRUBNKG? _____

9. ANSCP _____

10. DCSRMT _____

11. O,YINXTC? _____

12. DTNDYNRRS _____

13. RU4D9,RD? _____

14. URND12C _____

15. UR2BZ2CM _____

16. BLSD4NR _____

17. 1OU8Dπ _____

18. I8B4U _____

19. FDTVSOK, IMOK _____

20. DKNDSRS _____

98

72. TED'S RIPPED SHOPPING LIST

Shopping lists make the task of shopping much easier. Unfortunately for Ted, his shopping list was ripped in several places before he reached the supermarket. Only a few letters from each item to be purchased are left on the list. Fortunately, the items were listed in alphabetical order, which will help you to help Ted identify each item. Write the item's name in the space provided. No brand names are used.

1. _____ ppl

2. _____ para

3. _____ aco

4. _____ gels

5. _____ ueberr

6. _____ occol

7. _____ utte

8. _____ arro

9. _____ ndy

10. _____ hoco

11. _____ okie

12. _____ ggpl

13. _____ tuce

14. _____ rgar

15. _____ noo

16. _____ nges

17. _____ aches

18. _____ tato

19. _____ sou

20. _____ nach

21. _____ qua

22. _____ omato

23. _____ illas

24. _____ na

25. _____ termel

73. RECONSTRUCT A STORY CONTEST

The words below formerly made up five sentences from a story about a car problem. The words are listed alphabetically. You don't need to reconstruct the sentences as they originally appeared, but try your best to use as many of these words to form sentences. The winner is the student who has the fewest words left over after constructing sensible sentences.

a	costly	mechanic	the
a	down	near	the
an	drive	needed	the
and	fixed	new	the
automobile	he	new	to
battery	he	plug	today
Boston	hour	repairs	Walnut
broke	in	spark	were
car	John's	Street	will
car	less	than	yesterday

_____

_____

_____

_____

_____

_____

_____

Name _____ Date _____ Period _____

74. RECONSTRUCT ANOTHER STORY CONTEST

These forty-five words made up five sentences from a story about waking up late and its consequences. The words are listed alphabetically. You don't have to reconstruct the sentences exactly as they initially appeared, but do the best you can to use all the words on these lists. The student who has constructed sensible sentences and has the fewest number of words remaining is the winner!

after	I'll	now	supervises
alarm	in	on	the
also	late	other	the
clock	lateness	principal	there
detention	listen	punished	this
detention	me	school	to
fifth	morning	school	up
for	Mr.	served	was
fourteen	my	since	were
from	my	Smith	who
I	my	students	yesterday
			woke

_____

_____

_____

_____

_____

_____

_____

75. NO E'S PLEASE!

In the English translation of the novel, *A Void* by Georges Perec, the letter *e*, the most often used letter in the English alphabet, does not appear once! Here is a portion of Perec's first paragraph. After reading it, see if you can do the same with a 100-word paragraph in which you do not include the letter *e* a single time.

Incurably insomniac, Anton Vowl turns on a light. According to his watch, it's only 12:20. With a loud and languorous sigh, Vowl sits up, picks up his whodunit and idly scans a paragraph or two . . .

Here is your chance to write an "e-less" 100-word paragraph:

_____
_____
_____
_____
_____
_____
_____
_____
_____
_____
_____
_____
_____
_____
_____
_____
_____
_____
_____
_____
_____
_____
_____

Name _____ Date _____ Period _____

76. WORDS AND MESSAGES IN NUMBERS

In this activity numbers have replaced letters. As an example, the number 24 is the letter *w*. Thus, the number 24 is *w* in all the messages. The letters and numbers remain the same for all four messages. Write the letters beneath the numbers. Additionally, all of these messages have something in common. When you have deciphered all the messages, write the trait common to all messages in the space provided at the bottom of the page. A letter and number chart has been constructed for your convenience.

A B C D E F G H I J K L M N O P Q R S T U V W X Y Z

— —

Message 1: 8   11–8–18,   8   17–3–8–18,   8   25–8–18–8–3—   17–8–18–8–11–8

— — — — ,   — — — — ,   — — — — —   — — — — — —

Message 2: 21–5–26–17   10–18   18–10   17–26–5–21

— — — —   — —   — —   — — — —

Message 3: 8–19–3–26   24–8–21   7   26–2–26   7   21–8–24   26–3–19–8

— — — —   — — —   —   — — —   —   — — —   — — — —

Message 4: 21–7–5   10–18   8   17–10–5–8–5–10   17–8–18,   10–5–7–21

— — —   — —   —   — — — — — —   — — — ,   — — — —

Common trait: _____

77. HALF A PROVERB HERE, HALF A PROVERB THERE

Proverbs are life's little instructions. They can be quite helpful, if they are complete! The twenty proverbs that follow have been mixed up here. Join the proper parts together by writing the correct letter from Group Two next to the correct number from Group One. The first is done for you.

GROUP ONE

1. _M_ Be true to your teeth
2. ____ Bend the willow
3. ____ The early bird
4. ____ Flattery begets friends
5. ____ He who hesitates
6. ____ He who is born a fool
7. ____ Heavy burdens kill little people
8. ____ How the sapling bends
9. ____ It is better to smoke in this world
10. ____ It is easy to despise
11. ____ Lend money
12. ____ Many are called
13. ____ Never find your delight
14. ____ The shortest distance between two points
15. ____ Silence is sometimes
16. ____ A skillful cheater
17. ____ Slow and steady
18. ____ He who holds his peace and gathers stones
19. ____ The wise
20. ____ You can lead a student to college

GROUP TWO

(a) but few are chosen.
(b) but the truth begets enmity.
(c) but they make great ones.
(d) but you can't make him think.
(e) catches the worm.
(f) in another's misfortune.
(g) is a straight line.
(h) is lost.
(i) is never cured.
(j) is only once betrayed.
(k) lose a friend.
(l) needs no assistance.
(m) or they will be false to you.
(n) so grows the tree.
(o) than in the next.
(p) the severest critic.
(q) what you cannot get.
(r) while it's young.
(s) will find a time to throw them.
(t) wins the race.

78. CHANGE THE FIRST LETTER AND CHANGE THE WORD

With the exception of the first letter, the three answers in each question contain the same letters, in the same order. *Yellow*, *fellow*, and *mellow*, the answers to the first question show this pattern. Complete the remaining fourteen questions. Good luck!

1. a color y e l l o w
   a man f e l l o w
   a mood m e l l o w

2. to praise __ __ a __ __ __ r
   a large, shallow dish __ __ a __ __ __ r
   loud, sharp noise __ __ a __ __ __ r

3. a type of tree __ i __ __ o __
   a help for sleeping __ i __ __ o __
   a large wave __ i __ __ o __

4. an illumination device __ __ g __ __
   a struggle __ __ g __ __
   power __ __ g __ __

5. a concern __ __ __ __ y
   full of pity or sympathy __ __ __ __ y
   British word for truck __ __ __ __ y

6. sane __ __ u __ d
   circular __ __ u __ d
   lost's partner __ __ u __ d

7. to cover a wall __ a __ n __
   a very holy person __ a __ n __
   to sully __ a __ n __

8. to stop __ __ __ s __
   to rent __ __ __ s __
   to annoy or harass __ __ __ s __

78. CHANGE THE FIRST LETTER AND CHANGE THE WORD, CONTINUED

9. a fungi __ e __ __ __
    a holiday or commemoration __ e __ __ __
    large, four-footed animal __ e __ __ __

10. stripping off the skin __ __ __ __ n g
    concerned __ __ __ __ n g
    courageous __ __ __ __ n g

11. a color __ __ __ w __
    a headdress __ __ __ w __
    to die by suffocation in the water __ __ __ w __

12. a seat __ __ d __ __ e
    to row __ __ d __ __ e
    to walk with short steps __ __ d __ __ e

13. an angry look __ __ o w __ __
    a plant __ __ o w __ __
    one who breaks up the soil __ __ o w __ __

14. one who fixes __ __ __ __ e r
    one who loans __ __ __ __ e r
    one who forces an object to curve __ __ __ __ e r

15. an eating establishment __ __ n __ __
    one who digs coal or ore __ __ n __ __
    an ocean-cruising vehicle __ __ n __ __

Here is room for you to construct some more examples like those above.

79. LETTER PATTERNS

This is certainly an activity for stirring your brain. Each of the seven sentences asks you to identify its individual intriguing pattern of letters. Each sentence has a unique pattern. What clever or interesting letter patterns are found in these sentences? Write your answer in the space below the sentence.

1. A big Chilean dog emitted ferocious growls.

_____

2. Kennedy and Johnson were always debating tomorrow's warfare artfully.

_____

3. Starting Tuesday absolutely nobody demands his efforts!

_____

4. Many ride or land in vain, Gail.

_____

5. Bob senses that Alana did elude mom.

_____

6. Whenever Red describes seeing gnus, Sullivan naps.

_____

7. He rides above me.

_____

80. CHANGE A LETTER AND MAKE A NEW WORD

Start with a four-letter word. Change one letter to make a new four-letter word. Repeat the process for as many words as you can within five minutes. Write the words in the provided spaces. Compare your list with those of your classmates. Here is an example for you.

read - - dead - - deed - - feed - - feel - - peel - - reel - - reed - - heed - - hied - - tied - - tier - - bier - - Boer - - boar - - boat - - moat - - moan - - mean - - dean - - dear - - tear - - team - - beam - - seam - -

FIRST WORD	SECOND WORD	THIRD WORD	FOURTH WORD
_____	_____	_____	_____
_____	_____	_____	_____
_____	_____	_____	_____
_____	_____	_____	_____
_____	_____	_____	_____
_____	_____	_____	_____
_____	_____	_____	_____
_____	_____	_____	_____
_____	_____	_____	_____
_____	_____	_____	_____
_____	_____	_____	_____
_____	_____	_____	_____
_____	_____	_____	_____
_____	_____	_____	_____
_____	_____	_____	_____

81. THE NAME GAME

How good is your memory? Do you sometimes have trouble remembering names? Though this sounds like a commercial, it is only the introduction to the Name Game, an interesting way to remember names and improve your memory. To describe themselves, your classmates will think of one adjective that begins with the same letter as their names and then after the last student is finished, you will write as many of the adjectives as you remember. The second adjective space is there if time allows for a second round of adjectives. An example is given for you.

STUDENT	1ST ADJECTIVE	2ND ADJECTIVE
Anthony	agile	athletic
_____	_____	_____
_____	_____	_____
_____	_____	_____
_____	_____	_____
_____	_____	_____
_____	_____	_____
_____	_____	_____
_____	_____	_____
_____	_____	_____
_____	_____	_____
_____	_____	_____
_____	_____	_____
_____	_____	_____
_____	_____	_____
_____	_____	_____
_____	_____	_____
_____	_____	_____
_____	_____	_____
_____	_____	_____
_____	_____	_____
_____	_____	_____

82. THE WORD GAME

Forming a new word, but still keeping part of the old word, is the order of the day. Start off with a word, and then add another word to form a compound word or a common two-word expression. Keep the last part of the compound word or expression and add a new word to form yet another compound word or expression.

Here is an example starting with the word "check":

checkbook . . . bookcover . . . coverup . . . upshot . . . shotgun . . . gunman . . . manhole . . . holesaw . . . sawfly . . . flypaper . . . paperback . . . backfire . . . firehouse . . . housekey . . . keystone . . . stonewall . . . wallflower . . . flowerpot . . . potpie

Try your wordlists in the spaces below.

FIRST WORD LIST   **SECOND WORD LIST**   **THIRD WORD LIST**

Name _____ Date _____ Period _____

83. MAKING SENSE WITH YOUR SENSES

The way to a stronger vocabulary is to use words in your everyday experiences. You can do that in this activity by combining your five senses and appropriate adjectives. Restricting yourself to a single letter to start each word in the set, write a describing word next to each sense. See how well you can do with a number of different letters. The first set is done for you.

touch: amorous	touch: _____	touch: _____
taste: acid	taste: _____	taste: _____
sound: annoying	sound: _____	sound: _____
sight: awesome	sight: _____	sight: _____
smell: aromatic	smell: _____	smell: _____

touch: _____	touch: _____	touch: _____
taste: _____	taste: _____	taste: _____
sound: _____	sound: _____	sound: _____
sight: _____	sight: _____	sight: _____
smell: _____	smell: _____	smell: _____

touch: _____	touch: _____	touch: _____
taste: _____	taste: _____	taste: _____
sound: _____	sound: _____	sound: _____
sight: _____	sight: _____	sight: _____
smell: _____	smell: _____	smell: _____

84. CHARACTER POEMS

One of literature's purposes is to make the reader think. This activity's purpose is to make you think about the literary characters you've met in your readings. Select a character (or two or three) and create a character poem. Write the character's name vertically and then choose an appropriate adjective or noun that begins with that letter to describe the literary character. You can create character poems about historical figures, sports personalities, family members, or friends. Be prepared to explain your describing words. A character poem about Tom Sawyer is done here for you.

T . . . talkative

O . . . outgoing

M . . . memorable

S . . . sharp-witted

A . . . adventurous

W . . . whimsical

Y . . . youthful

E . . . energetic

R . . . resourceful

_____

_____

_____

_____

_____

_____

_____

_____

_____

_____

_____

_____

_____

_____

85. THE RIGHT WRITE THING TO TOO TWO DO DUE DEW

Your eyes are not playing tricks on you. The title is deliberately confusing to match the type of work you will do here. Homonyms, words that have the same pronunciation as another word but a different meaning and spelling, are the answers to each question. The first letter of each homonym is given. Fill in the remaining letters. The first answer is done for you.

1. We were t <u>a</u> <u>u</u> <u>g</u> <u>h</u> t that the rope should be t <u>a</u> u t.

2. Yvonne and her friends were quite b __ __ __ __ with the different b __ __ __ __ games they played while it was raining.

3. He looked in v __ __ __ for the hidden weather v __ __ __ __ .

4. The player was f __ __ __ __ fifty dollars unless they f __ __ __ more incriminating evidence against him.

5. Y __ __ can find the e __ __ near the y __ __ tree.

6. He hurt his t __ __ when we tried to t __ __ him to safety.

7. Sam thought it was g __ __ __ __ that he found the prize under the g __ __ __ __ __ .

8. Tom wanted to h __ __ __ a taxi since he didn't feel h __ __ __ __ .

9. Raymond a __ __ at e __ __ __ __ o'clock.

10. Donna felt p __ __ __ when she put her hand through the window p __ __ __ __ .

11. Georgia told us an interesting t __ __ __ about the rabbit's t __ __ __ __ .

12. None of the forecasters knew w __ __ __ __ __ __ the w __ __ __ __ __ __ __ was going to change in the next twenty-four hours.

13. The horse's g __ __ __ changed when she neared the g __ __ __ .

14. The m __ __ __ m __ __ __ the house look very clean before the company arrived.

15. He let out a g __ __ __ __ when the doctor said he had not g __ __ __ __ at all during the year.

16. Geraldine had the good s __ __ __ __ to detect the unusual s __ __ __ __ __ that came from the room.

17. Since the p __ __ __ was so heavy, she looked p __ __ __ after picking it up.

18. After trying to completely w __ __ __ __ out the towels, Drew realized he had misplaced his r __ __ __ .

19. Both Ursula and Frankie let out a w __ __ __ when they saw that the w __ __ __ __ was so near their boat.

20. George started to b __ __ __ __ a sweat when his car's b __ __ __ __ did not immediately catch.

Section Four

LOGIC
AND
REASONING

86. THE ART OF ORGANIZING

How much time is wasted looking for a pair of pants, a set of keys, a shoe? Organizing and knowing where things can be found is a wonderful time-saver.

The following ten situations demand good organizational skills. Show how you would organize each of the following situations. Write your responses on a separate piece of paper.

1. Your mom and dad feel they waste too much time searching for certain records from their rock-and-roll oldies collection. You have been asked to put these 376 record albums in some orderly fashion.

2. How would you organize your English class notebook since you do so many different types of topics in that class?

3. Organize the more than 200 books on your family's bookshelves.

4. Arrange the items in your basement, garage, or shed in some orderly fashion.

5. How would you organize the types of bills that your family must pay each month?

6. Over the years you have collected many items from your days at school. Show a plan to organize these items.

7. How would you arrange the various types of cards in a card shop?

8. Make the supermarket shopping experience faster and easier. Organize the items by various aisles and/or departments.

9. Arrange the items in an automotive parts store.

10. Organize the items found in a brochure about your town or city.

87. WHY IT HAS THE NAME IT DOES

Did you realize that you own a bridge? Well, if you think about it, your nose has a bridge. Why is it called a bridge? That is your first question in this exercise. Here are other names associated with your body. In the spaces provided, write why each has the name it does.

1. bridge of your nose: _____

2. handlebar mustache: _____

3. sourpuss: _____

4. sideburns: _____

5. the ball of your foot: _____

6. eye tooth: _____

7. Adam's apple: _____

8. bowlegs: _____

9. funny bone: _____

10. pigeon-toed: _____

11. index finger: _____

12. kneecap: _____

13. wisdom tooth: _____

14. Achilles tendon: _____

15. fallen arches of the feet: _____

16. forehead: _____

17. crown of your head: _____

18. pot belly: _____

19. barrel-chested: _____

20. forearm: _____

21. lantern jawed: _____

22. cherubic face: _____

Name _____ Date _____ Period _____

88. A SCORE OF ANALOGIES

In the space provided, write an analogy similar to the given one. Be ready to explain your analogy.

1. duke: duchess _____

2. investigate: crime _____

3. beret: head _____

4. shovel: dig _____

5. ghastly: nauseate _____

6. company: commander _____

7. mumble: talk _____

8. thermometer: temperature _____

9. priest: ordination _____

10. outlast: endurance _____

11. dwarf: giant _____

12. aria: musical _____

13. throttle: gauge _____

14. nutshell: summary _____

15. ruffian: kind _____

16. incorrigible: obedient _____

17. vile: attractive _____

18. exonerate: defendant _____

19. misdemeanor: felony _____

20. thief: purloin _____

89. SEEMINGLY SENSELESS EQUATIONS THAT DO MAKE SENSE!

If you were told that 5 + 5 = 2, you might think you were going crazy. Yet, you know that 5 fingers + 5 fingers = 2 hands, so this seemingly senseless equation does make sense! You're just looking at a common idea in an uncommon way. Write your answers in the spaces provided. Make up five equations of your own in the remaining space.

1. 365 1/4 = 1 _____

2. 2 + 12 = 1 _____

3. 11 + 30 = 1 _____

4. 168 = 1 _____

5. 1 − 60 = 23 _____

6. C = LX + XL _____

7. 52 = 1 _____

8. 1760 + 5280 = 2 _____

9. 720 − 2 = 1/6 _____

10. 25 − 60 = 1 _____

90. MYSTERIOUS SEQUENCES

Here are ten groups of the first letters from rather common sequences. So if you saw *S*, *M*, *T*, *W*, *T*, *F*, *S*, you would know that this group is the days of the week. Write your answers in the appropriate spaces. Stump your classmates by creating some of your own.

1. _____ J, F, M, A, M, J, J, A, S, O, N, D

2. _____ O, T, T, F, F, S, S, E, N, T

3. _____ R, O, Y, G, B, I, V

4. _____ M, V, E, M, J, S, U, N, P

5. _____ W, A, J, M, M, A, J

6. _____ A, T, G, C, L, V, L, S, S, C, A, P

7. _____ I, F, Y, M

8. _____ A, B, G, D, E, Z, E, T, I, K

9. _____ E, G, B, D, F

10. _____ N, P, V, A, A, P, C, I

Name _____ Date _____ Period _____

91. WRITING THE RIGHT WORDS

A writer's task is to make his or her story believable. Often this involves selecting the appropriate word to fit the mood, setting, or character. In this process the author must choose the exact word to convey exactly what is intended.

    In this activity you, as the author, are asked to fill in the blank space(s) to accurately convey the specified mood. No word may be used more than once in the activity. Be ready to support why you chose those words over other possible selections. Consider using a dictionary or thesaurus. The first one is already done for you.

1. (horror) The <u>threatening</u> figure <u>emerged</u> from the <u>dark</u> and <u>ominous</u> expanse.

2. (joy) After the _____ was _____, the _____ team members _____.

3. (anger) As he _____ the door, he _____ to his enemy.

4. (suspicion) Never before had she _____ in such a manner, _____ that she would not _____ again.

5. (sadness) The _____ couple, _____ by their loss, _____ together near the water's edge.

6. (anticipation) Hardly able to _____, Marilyn felt _____ and _____ about the _____ moment.

7. (indecision) _____ his options, Frank _____ that he had never _____ such an _____ before this.

8. (panic) Barely able to _____, the driver _____ the car _____ the _____ _____.

9. (confidence) Without _____, Pat, the girl who _____ the _____, approached the _____ _____ly.

10. (tranquility) Such a _____ setting, with its _____ _____ and _____ , was perfect for _____ .

92. COUNT ME IN

In each exercise, the four members share a common bond. Write the group's common identity in the space provided. The first is done for you.

1. _____odd numbers_____   1, 3, 15, 17

2. _____   May, August, January, October

3. _____   turnpike, highway, freeway, expressway

4. _____   Harvard, Penn, Yale, Dartmouth

5. _____   cabbage, onion, asparagus, turnip

6. _____   backgammon, checkers, chess, monopoly

7. _____   Buddhism, Hinduism, Islam, Protestantism

8. _____   level, radar, madam, tenet

9. _____   humerus, femur, tibia, ulna

10. _____   da Gama, Columbus, Magellan, Raleigh

11. _____   adjective, adverb, conjunction, pronoun

12. _____   Algeria, Chad, Mozambique, Sudan

13. _____   pitcher, catcher, shortstop, outfielder

14. _____   Mozart, Bach, Verdi, Tchaikovsky

15. _____   jeté, allongé, plié, fondu

16. _____   Louisa May Alcott, Jane Austen, Pearl S. Buck, Margaret Mitchell

17. _____   Artemision at Ephesus, The Colossus of Rhodes, The Pyramids of Egypt, The Hanging Gardens of Babylon

18. _____   alpha, beta, gamma, delta

93. THIS IS TO THIS

Analogies show the similarities between two words. "Apple is to fruit" is the same as "man is to human being" since each *first* word is a type of the second word. Fill in the missing word in each of these analogies. Some analogies may have more than one answer.

1. tall is to height as heavy is to _____

2. sister is to woman as brother is to _____

3. wig is to hair as denture is to _____

4. speech is to oral as sight is to _____

5. Albany is to New York as Boston is to _____

6. purity is to white as envy is to _____

7. baseball is to bat as tennis is to _____

8. king is to queen as duke is to _____

9. crimson is to red as azure is to _____

10. human is to heart as motor is to _____

11. schedule is to travel as menu is to _____

12. leg is knee as arm is to _____

13. playwright is to actor as composer is to _____

14. exile is to deport as tenant is to _____

15. Aristotle is to Greece as Confucius is to _____

16. chapter is to novel as act is to _____

17. tie is to neck as ring is to _____

18. Bill is to William as Debbie is to _____

19. telephone is to area code as mail is to _____

20. ruler is to inches as thermometer is to _____

Name _____ Date _____ Period _____

94. SERIOUS ABOUT SERIES

How well can you figure out the arrangement of numbers? Each of the following number groups is arranged in some order. Write the next number in the series and be ready to explain why you selected that number.

1. 1, 3, 5, 7, 9, _____
2. 2, 4, 6, 8, 10, _____
3. 3, 9, 27, 81, _____
4. 164, 82, 41, 20.5, _____
5. 1, 4, 9, 16, 25, _____
6. 1, 3, 6, 10, _____
7. 2, 4, 5, 10, 11, 22, 23, 46, 47, _____
8. 884, 221, 55.25, 13.8125, _____
9. 3, 12, 11, 44, 43, 172, 171, _____
10. 6, 5, 8, 7, 10, 9, 12, _____
11. 5, 7, 14, 16, 32, 34, 68, _____
12. 1/27, 1/9, 1/3, 1, _____
13. 8, 12, 12, 16, 16, 20, _____
14. 4, 11, 13, 20, 22, _____
15. 1/16, 1/32, 1/64, _____
16. 63, 59, 57, 53, 51, 47, _____
17. 1/5, 3/5, 9/5, 27/5, _____
18. .16, .32, .64, 1.28, _____
19. .04, .08, .16, .32, _____
20. 4, 3, 15, 14, 70, 69, 345, _____

95. AND THEN THIS HAPPENED

Sometimes a discovery or invention causes other events to take place. What are several effects of the telephone's invention? These and other questions will test your ability to see what effects occurred because of an invention or discovery. List your reasons in the spaces provided.

INVENTION/DISCOVERY

1. The telephone

2. The computer

3. The wheel

4. Electricity

5. Vaccines

6. Money

7. Chemotherapy

EFFECTS

communication became quicker, easier, more convenient, jobs, factories are built, environment may be less attractive because of telephone poles, written communication is lessened

_____
_____
_____
_____
_____
_____
_____
_____
_____
_____
_____
_____
_____
_____
_____
_____
_____
_____

96. THE SCRAMBLED-UP TRIOS

The words found within fifteen common trios have been scrambled up. A clue to help you identify each member of the trio has been given to you. Thus if the clue reads, "Words to the wise," and the scrambled up trio members listed are: ptos lkoo ilsent, the answer would be stop, look, and listen. Write your answers in the spaces provided.

1. Clue: America's colors
   dre   wethi   lbeu

   _____ _____ _____

2. Clue: A day at the races
   inw   palec   hsow

   _____ _____ _____

3. Clue: Old-time school subjects
   raiden'   rgiitn'   rimhtietc'

   _____ _____ _____

4. Clue: Do you believe it all?
   koho   ienl   iesrnk

   _____ _____ _____

5. Clue: C.S. Lewis's trio
   oiln   iwcth   awedobrr

   _____ _____ _____

6. Clue: A flavorful trio
   aivanll   hcoclaoet   tasrweyrbr

   _____ _____ _____

7. Clue: How some obtain things
   bge   rborow   leats

   _____ _____ _____

8. Clue: Girls' names or months of the year
   plair   yma   eunj

   _____ _____ _____

96. THE SCRAMBLED-UP TRIOS, CONTINUED

9. Clue: Girls' names or virtues
afith   peoh   ahrytci

_____ _____ _____

10. Clue: The times are a 'changin
psta   rspenet   ufrute

_____ _____ _____

11. Clue: A handsome man's qualities
ltal   krda   adhenosm

_____ _____ _____

12. Clue: The French connection
lbieytr   euqaiylt   fieyntarrt

_____ _____ _____

Now make up some of your trios in the space below.

Name _____ Date _____ Period _____

97. MOMENTS IN TIME

Could Babe Ruth have used an electric shaver in 1927, the year he hit 60 home runs? No, he could not have done so since the electric shaver was manufactured a few years later. Now that's a close shave! Here are some other events that could (or could not) have happened. Using your knowledge of historical dates and events, write "Yes" next to the possible occurrences and "No" next to those that could not have happened.

1. ____ Could John F. Kennedy have seen Neil Armstrong walk on the moon?

2. ____ Could Elvis Presley have sung the song "Thriller" along with singer Michael Jackson?

3. ____ Could basketball player Michael Jordan have witnessed the collapse of the Berlin Wall?

4. ____ Could George Washington have spoken with Napoleon?

5. ____ Could poet Emily Dickinson have watched an organized baseball game?

6. ____ Could the inventor of the printing press, Gutenberg, have printed Shakespeare's *Romeo and Juliet*?

7. ____ Could Columbus have attended Magellan's burial?

8. ____ Could a dog born in the middle of the nineteenth century have had a rabies immunization?

9. ____ Could Marilyn Monroe have attended the 1969 Woodstock Festival?

10. ____ Could Ronald Reagan have spoken with Charlie Chaplin?

11. ____ Could Mark Twain have read Lucy C. Montgomery's *Anne of Green Gables*?

12. ____ Could Indira Gandhi, if invited, have attended the swearing in of the first woman on the U.S. Supreme Court, Sandra Day O'Connor?

13. ____ Could Richard Nixon have listened to a CD?

98. IS IT POSSIBLE THAT . . .?

It is interesting to think about certain historical possibilities. Trying to figure out whether certain people could have witnessed certain events calls for intelligent thinking. Here are ten situations. If they could have happened, write "Yes" in the space. If not, write "No."

1. ____ Could Babe Ruth have attended Lou Gehrig's funeral?

2. ____ Could George Washington have sung "Auld Lang Syne" while President of the United States?

3. ____ Could dynamite have been used in the Civil War?

4. ____ Could Tchaikovsky have traveled by zeppelin to perform his *The Nutcracker* ballet?

5. ____ Could Mike Tyson have boxed Muhammad Ali for the heavyweight championship?

6. ____ Could Shakespeare have used a fork while eating?

7. ____ Could Leonardo Da Vinci have used a pocket handkerchief?

8. ____ Could Henry VIII have used a black-lead pencil?

9. ____ Could Marco Polo have traveled on a toll road in England?

10. ____ Could Jackie Robinson, the first Black to play in major league baseball, have watched a game having a designated hitter?

Name _____ Date _____ Period _____

99. A COUNTRY'S VALUES THROUGH ITS CURRENCY

This exercise can be a lot of fun. It is very important that you pretend that you know nothing about the people of this culture whose coin or dollar you've found. Let's see how good you are at making assumptions and being able to back them up with solid evidence. Use coins or bills from any culture to complete this exercise.

1. What coin or dollar bill do you have in front of you? _____

2. What are some of the objects or persons found on the front of this coin or bill? Please list them. (Fill in as many as you can.)

_____   _____   _____

_____   _____   _____

_____   _____   _____

3. What are some of the objects or persons found on the reverse side of this coin or bill? Please list them. (Fill in as many as you can.)

_____   _____   _____

_____   _____   _____

_____   _____   _____

4. Based on these objects and persons you've listed, what statements can you make about this culture? Be able to support your statements. Please list your statements below.

Statement 1:

_____

Statement 2:

_____

Statement 3:

_____

Statement 4:

_____

Statement 5:

_____

Compare your answers with those of your classmates.

Name _____ Date _____ Period _____

100. METS, JETS, NETS, AND OTHER SPORTS SETS

You don't have to be an avid sports fan to do well in this exercise. Ever wonder why certain professional sports teams have the names they do? Why are the Mets the Mets, the Jets the Jets, and so forth? Does it have to do with the city, the sport, or another reason? List the reason for the team's name in the space provided. Please remember that some teams have moved from one city to the present one listed. Their names may be because of their affiliation with the original city.

1. Montreal Canadiens: _____

2. Washington Capitals: _____

3. Philadelphia Flyers: _____

4. New York Islanders: _____

5. Toronto Maple Leafs: _____

6. Vancouver Canucks: _____

7. Edmonton Oilers: _____

8. Ottawa Senators: _____

9. Quebec Nordiques: _____

10. Philadelphia 76ers: _____

11. Boston Celtics: _____

12. Dallas Mavericks: _____

13. Indiana Pacers: _____

14. Los Angeles Lakers: _____

15. Orlando Magic: _____

16. New Jersey Nets: _____

17. New York Knickerbockers: _____

101. A PART IS MISSING

Complete these combinations of words by filling in the *same* word that belongs with each word in the group. Thus if the words were _____ club, _____ review, and _____ value, the word "book" completes all three correctly to have book club, book review, and book value. For each exercise, write the correct word in the spaces provided.

1. _____ buckle, _____ coat, _____ down

2. _____ shot, _____ spot, _____ water

3. _____ rites, _____ straw, _____ word

4. _____ bug, _____ digger, _____ dust

5. _____ bomb, _____ picker, _____ tomato

6. _____ dribble, _____ jeopardy, _____ play

7. _____ cream, _____ foo young, _____ roll

8. _____ day, _____ event, _____ goal

9. _____ aid, _____ base, _____ family

10. _____ guard, _____ roll, _____ society

11. _____ alert, _____ carpet, _____ herring

12. _____ dance, _____ deal, _____ root

13. _____ elephant, _____ flag, _____ knight

14. _____ change, _____ intestine, _____ talk

15. _____ fever, _____ jacket, _____ journalism

102. KNOW US BY OUR SLOGANS

Here are twenty companies whose slogans tell us something about what each company does. Match the companies with their slogans. Each can be used only once.

1. ____ Candy's Candy Company
2. ____ Family Tires
3. ____ Ace Accounting Firm
4. ____ Creative Comics
5. ____ Fitness Fun
6. ____ All-Wet Pool Installers
7. ____ All-Star Baseball Camp
8. ____ Finest Cars Dealer
9. ____ Arctic Air Conditioners
10. ____ Easy Rid Exterminators

11. ____ Sherry's Beauty Salon
12. ____ Well Diggers
13. ____ Alarm Security Systems
14. ____ Ed's Eyeglass Center
15. ____ Jack's Junk Cars
16. ____ Wally's Windows
17. ____ Sal's Shoe Repairs
18. ____ Bob's Brakes
19. ____ Aerial Photographers
20. ____ Mike's Marine Supplies

TOWER'S ANTI-CRAMP PENHOLDER PAT'D. FEB 21. 66?

a. Take Us for a Ride!

b. You Can Count on Us!

c. How Sweet It Is!

d. You'll See the Difference!

e. Jump In and Enjoy!

f. Take Us Hook, Line and Sinker!

g. Chill Out!

h. Our Books Are for Real!

i. We'll Make You Wreckless!

j. The Right Way to the Right Weight!

k. Your Eye in the Sky!

l. Stop Here!

m. We See What You Can't!

n. Take Our Pitch the Distance!

o. The Best Panes You'll See!

p. We're the Best Heels!

q. We Do the Hole Thing!

r. A Hair-Raising Experience!

s. The Road Hugging People!

t. Keep Your Uncles! We Want Your ants!

Name _____ Date _____ Period _____

103. MIXED-UP ADVERTISEMENTS

Andy, the local newspaper's advertisement department manager, has a problem. Unfortunately, he has mixed up the companies and their advertising information. He knows that Ozzie's Jewelry Outlet should not have an ad reading, "The best tires for your truck." Help Andy place the right information with the correct company by matching the ads with their information. Each can only be used once. The first one is done for you.

1. <u>b</u>   Bob's Auto Repair
2. ____ Shane's Opticals
3. ____ A-1 Construction
4. ____ Town Florists
5. ____ Gem Jewelers
6. ____ Nails-R-Us
7. ____ The Pet Depot
8. ____ Romance Restaurant
9. ____ Larry's Landscaping
10. ____ Today's Men's Clothiers

11. ____ Kay's Camera Store
12. ____ Best Seating Gallery
13. ____ All-Star Appliances
14. ____ Better Savings Bank
15. ____ Toys for Tots
16. ____ Gary's Golfing Gallery
17. ____ Kent's Auto Mall
18. ____ Allyson's Antiques
19. ____ Dr. Pauline Smythe
20. ____ Lance's Limos

a. Flowerbeds weeded and maintained
b. Axle replacement
c. Large capacity dryer with 6 cycles
d. European designer suits
e. Crowns and Braces
f. 50% off all frames in stock
g. $3000 trade-in and 24-month lease
h. Interest Rate, Account Balance and Minimum Opening Deposit
i. 14X zoom and color viewfinder
j. Chicken and Broccoli Francaise
k. 1-carat diamond
l. Preschool Toys, Infant Toys, and Action Figures
m. Woods, Irons, and Carts
n. 30′ dormer or 12′ by 12′ extension
o. Authentic 1753 hutch
p. Manicure and Pedicure
q. Flea and Tick Products
r. Super sofas and fabrics
s. Prom and Wedding specials; Can accommodate 8 comfortably
t. Dozens of carnations

Name _____ Date _____ Period _____

104. DECODING THE MESSAGE

Bob and his college friends are at the Saturday afternoon nationally televised football game. They have made up a sign with a message to the dear folks at home. In a rather clever way, they have concealed their message to home. All the letters in the message have been assigned a number. Your job is to figure out the most appropriate message they are sending by selecting the correct sequence of letters from the message. Circle the correct letter sequence and then write their message in the space marked "Concealed Message."

Their message reads:

W h e n e v e r   D o m   w o r e   m y   o n e   h a t,
1 2 3 4 5 6 7 8   9 10 11   12 13 14 15   16 17   18 19 20   21 22 23

y o u'd   l a u g h.
24 25 26 27   28 29 30 31 32

Which is the correct sequence of their concealed message?

(a) 2, 3, 4, 5, 6, 7, 8, 19, 20, 22, 23, 28, 29, 31.

(b) 14, 15, 22, 9, 1, 19, 6, 7, 8, 17, 28, 29, 27, 24.

(c) 5, 6, 7, 8, 24, 9, 10, 13, 14, 17, 18, 26, 27, 30, 31.

(d) 2, 3, 8, 15, 16, 18, 22, 23, 30, 31, 32!

(e) 1, 2, 3, 4, 5, 6, 7, 8, 17, 18, 19, 20, 21, 22, 27, 28, 30, 31.

(f) 1, 3, 4, 5, 7, 9, 11, 13, 14, 15, 16, 18, 19, 20, 24.

(g) 9, 10, 19, 25, 23, 20, 4, 6, 24, 14, 15, 27, 13, 14, 15.

CONCEALED MESSAGE: _____

Section Five

MATH

Name _____ Date _____ Period _____

105. THEY ALL ADD UP THE SAME

Using the numbers 1, 2, 3, 4, 5, 6, 7, 8, and 9, place the numbers in the proper boxes within the square so that each of the rows—vertical, horizontal, and diagonal—adds up to 15. Use each number once only.

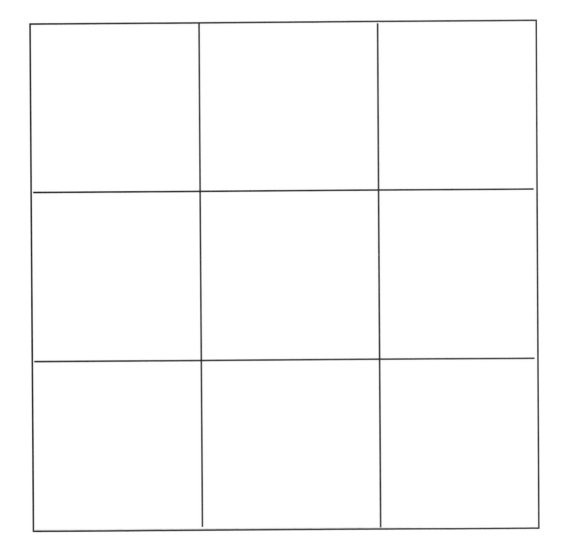

IO6. NUMBER STUMPER

This activity is bound to get your gray matter moving. Using the clues given for each number, figure out the number answer for each question. If you figure the answer out after two clues, give yourself two points. If you figure it out after three clues, give yourself one point. But if you're wrong after either clue, deduct the same number of points! Here is an example to get you started.

Example: Clue 1: It is an even two-digit number.

   2: The difference between its digits is 1.

   3: When the two digits are multiplied, the product is 12.

The answer is <u>34</u>

1.   Clue 1: It is an odd two-digit number.

   2: The sum of its digits is 8.

   3: The sum of the squares of its digits is 50.

   Answer: _____

2.   Clue 1: It is an odd two-digit number.

   2: The product of its two digits is 24.

   3: When the second digit is subtracted from the first, the difference is 5.

   Answer: _____

3.   Clue 1: It is an even two-digit number.

   2: One-half the number is 5 more than the number of days in a fortnight.

   3: The sum of the squares of the two digits is 73.

   Answer: _____

4.   Clue 1: It is an odd two-digit number.

   2: The difference of the two digits is 5.

   3: The difference in the squares of the two digits is 45.

   Answer: _____

5.   Clue 1: It is an even two-digit number.

                        2: The sum of the two digits is 10.

                        3: The difference of the two digits is 2.

                        Answer: _____

6.   Clue 1: It is an odd two-digit number.

                        2: The sum of the two digits is 10.

                        3: The difference of the two digits is 0.

                        Answer: _____

7.   Clue 1: It is a palindromic three-digit number.

                        2: The sum of the digits' squares is 99.

                        3: The sum of its digits is 15.

                        Bonus Clue: Turn me upside down and I spell a woman's name.

                        Answer: _____

In the space below, make up three problems like the ones above.

107. LARGEST TO SMALLEST

Arrange the members of each group in order from the largest to the smallest. Write your answers in the spaces provided.

1. 1/16, .41, 7/8, 3/7, 1 _____

2. 9/14, cube root of 125, square root of 49, 16/2, 4/3 _____

3. 8/3, . . . 1/36, 1/3, 1/6, 2/9 _____

4. cube root of 343, 42/7, 3 squared, 2 × 3/2, 25/5 _____

5. square root of 19, 4.2 squared, 6 times the square root of 9, 55/3, 101/5.64 _____

_____

6. 64 × .25, 16 divided by .98, 19 divided by 1.2, 15.9 × 1.2, 71 divided by 3.64 _____

_____

7. 39 divided by 14, 22 divided by 7, 25 divided by 8, 29 divided by 9, 41 divided by 12.4

_____

_____

8. 7.9 × 6.6, 7.1 × 7.9, 7.2 × 7.8, 7.3 × 7.7, 7.4 × 7.6 _____

9. 17 divided by 4, 21 divided by 5, 25 divided by 6, 29 divided by 7, 33 divided by 8 __

_____

10. 23 divided by 8, 26 divided by 9, 8 divided by 3, 14 divided by 5, 41 divided by 14 __

_____

Name _____ Date _____ Period _____

108. SEQUENCING TO ONE

If you perform the operations in each of the following sequences correctly, the answer is always 1. The "certain number" that begins each sequence is always a whole number. No "certain number" is greater than 10.

Here is an example to get you going:

Multiply a certain number by 3 . . . take away 4 . . . divide by 2. The answer is **2**. 2 times 3 is 6 . . . 6 minus 4 is 2 . . . 2 divided by 2 is 1. Write your answers in the appropriate spaces.

GROUP ONE

(Hint: The answers to the Group One questions add up to 30.)

A. _____ Multiply a certain number by 7 . . . divide by 14.

B. _____ Multiply a certain number by 9 . . . divide by 27 . . . subtract 2

C. _____ Divide a certain number by 5 . . . multiply by 1/2

D. _____ Add 3 to a certain number . . . subtract 8

E. _____ Subtract a certain number from 10 . . . subtract 5 . . . subtract 1

GROUP TWO

(Hint: The answers to the Group Two questions add up to 25.)

F. _____ Multiply a certain number by 3 . . . divide by 3 . . . divide by 5

G. _____ Multiply a certain number by 3 . . . subtract 11 . . . divide by 2 . . . minus 4 . . .

H. _____ Double a certain number . . . divide by 8, . . . multiply by 1/2

I. _____ Triple a certain number . . . divide by 3 . . . subtract 3

J. _____ Quadruple a certain number . . . divide by 4

GROUP THREE

(Hint: The answers to the Group Three questions add up to 28.)

K. _____ Double a number . . . divide by 5 . . . minus 3

L. _____ Divide a certain number by 2 . . . multiply by 1/3

M. _____ Square a number . . . minus 20 . . . divide by 5

N. _____ Add 2 to a certain number . . . multiply by 2 . . . divide by 6 . . . minus 1

O. _____ Cube a certain number . . . divide by 9 . . . minus 2

143

109. COUNTING YOUR CHANGE

Here are some money problems that will test your ability to think quickly and accurately. In column A is the amount of money; in column B is the number of coins that make up that first column's amount. In the space provided under the column C heading, write the number of coins that make up column A's amount. The coins are quarters (*Q*), dimes (*D*), nickels (*N*), and pennies (*P*). The first one is already done for you.

COLUMN A	COLUMN B	COLUMN C Q D N P
1. 25¢	5	0 0 5 0
2. 35¢	7	_____
3. 33¢	8	_____
4. 46¢	5	_____
5. 56¢	7	_____
6. 17¢	4	_____
7. 43¢	6	_____
8. 29¢	7	_____
9. 54¢	8	_____
10. 57¢	7	_____
11. 48¢	7	_____
12. 34¢	8	_____
13. 59¢	9	_____
14. 55¢	5	_____
15. 88¢	7	_____
16. 75¢	5	_____
17. 47¢	5	_____
18. 36¢	5	_____
19. 32¢	4	_____
20. 42¢	5	_____

Name _____ Date _____ Period _____

IIO. FIGURING OUT THE CHANGE

Below are three groups of coins. Your challenge: As coins are shuffled in and out of these groups, see if you can figure out how much money is in each group each time. Each numbered challenge tells you some necessary information and then asks you to fill in the other bits of information to solve each problem. Pennies, nickels, dimes, and quarters are the coins used. Write your answers in the spaces provided. The first group is done for you.

	GROUP 1	GROUP 2	GROUP 3	TOTAL
1.	2 coins	_3_ coins	4 coins	9 coins
	11¢	16¢	_12¢_	39¢

The total number of dimes in the three groups is _____.

2.	__ coins	4 coins	5 coins	12 coins
	45¢	26¢	__¢	89¢

The total number of nickels in the three groups is _____.

3.	7 coins	__ coins	3 coins	15 coins
	__¢	31¢	35¢	91¢

The total number of quarters in the three groups is _____.

4.	__ coins	5 coins	5 coins	14 coins
	37¢	27¢	__¢	$1.10

The total number of pennies in the three groups is _____.

5.	4 coins	__ coins	4 coins	14 coins
	31¢	43¢	__¢	$1.15

The total number of quarters in the three groups is _____.

6.	5 coins	5 coins	__ coins	16 coins
	31¢	__¢	67¢	$1.16

The total number of dimes in the three groups is _____.

III. THE BIG LEAGUES' SPRING TRAINING LEAGUE

Sy Sidney, the sensational sportswriter, wants to write an article about the Big Leagues. However, he has trouble with figuring out percentages. So here's where you come in. Help Sy with information he will use in the next article by answering the following percentage questions. Batter up!

TEAM	WINS	LOSSES	WINNING PCT.
Boston Red Sox	10	2	.833
Kansas City Royals	9	3	.750
Chicago White Sox	7	5	.583
California Angels	6	6	.500
Montreal Expos	4	8	.333
Minnesota Twins	1	11	.083

1. If all the teams win one and lose one of their next two games, which team will still have the same percentage? _____

2. If Minnesota wins the next four games, what is its new winning percentage? _____

3. How many consecutive wins would California have to have before its winning percentage reaches .650 or better? _____

4. Both California and Chicago win their next three games. By how much has the difference in their winning percentages changed? _____

5. Kansas City wins six of their next thirteen games. What is the team's new winning percentage? _____

6. How many consecutive wins does Montreal need before it reaches .500? _____

7. Which team has won 3⁄4 of its games? _____

8. Which team has won 1⁄2 of its games? _____

9. Which team has won 5⁄6 of its games? _____

10. If Montreal continues at its same pace, how many games will the team win out of their next twelve? _____

11. If Minnesota continues to win at the same pace, how many wins will they have after a total of 36 games? _____

12. If Kansas City and Boston play each other for six consecutive games and Kansas City wins all of the games, what will its winning percentage be? _____

13. California wins their next three and Kansas City loses its next two. Whose percentage is higher and by how much? _____

14. If the season consists of a total of twenty games, can Minnesota reach the .500 mark? _____

15. If the season consists of 21 games, can Boston fall below the .500 mark? _____

112. THE PERCENTAGES ARE WITH YOU

Using the table of figures below, answer these questions dealing with a school district's population. Percentages should be rounded off to the nearest whole number.

GROUP	NUMBER	BOYS	GIRLS
Elementary	1378	756	622
Middle School	2231	1098	1133
High School	4339	2231	2108
Total	7948	4085	3863

1. Boys make up what percent of the entire school district's population? _____

2. Girls make up what percent of the entire school district's population? _____

3. The elementary school population is what percent of the entire district's population? _____

4. The middle school population is what percent of the entire district's population? _____

5. The high school population is what percent of the entire district's population? _____

6. Elementary boys make up what percent of the entire district's population? _____

7. Middle school girls make up what percent of the entire district's population? _____

8. High school girls make up what percent of the entire district's population? _____

9. The middle school boys make up what percent of the district's boys' population? _____

10. If the elementary population increases by 250 and the middle school and high school populations remain constant, what percent of the entire district's population will the elementary school population then be? _____

11. If the population of the high school drops by 347, what percent of the district's population will the high school then be? _____

12. If 314 new girls enter the school district, what percent of the entire school district will the girls constitute? _____

113. THE CENTURY CLUB

The following three groups all have something in common—if you have correctly figured out each percent problem. Write your answers in the spaces provided and then on the line marked "COMMON," tell what is shared by all three groups.

GROUP ONE

1. _____ is 11% of 100.
2. _____ is 40% of 80.
3. _____ is 25% of 80.
4. _____ is 15% of 60.
5. _____ is 50% of 56.
6. _____ is the total of the answers in numbers 1–5.

GROUP TWO

1. _____ is 42% of 50.
2. _____ is 12% of 75.
3. _____ is 8% of 300.
4. _____ is 35% of 60.
5. _____ is 50% of 50.
6. _____ is the total of the answers in numbers 1–5.

GROUP THREE

1. _____ is 80% of 40.
2. _____ is 140% of 25.
3. _____ is 2% of 200.
4. _____ is 15% of 40.
5. _____ is 46% of 50.
6. _____ is the total of the answers in numbers 1–5.

COMMON: _____

Name _____ Date _____ Period _____

114. A TAXING SITUATION

It's important when computing the cost of items that we include the tax. A clothing item priced at $100 quickly becomes $110 when the 10% tax is included in the final cost. Here are some real situations that you might encounter in your daily life. Write your answer to each problem in the space provided.

1. If a CD costs $15 and the tax is 8%, what's the final cost? _____

2. If the shoes are priced at $55 and the tax is 7%, what's the final cost? _____

3. You are asked to pay your share of the phone bill. If your phone charges are $33 and the tax is 6%, what is your cost of the bill? _____

4. You and your friends receive a lunch bill for $22.50 before the tax is included. The tax in your state is 8%. What is the total cost when the tax is included? _____

5. Your friend's birthday present costs you $22. The tax, which is included in the final price of the present, is 10%. What is the cost of the item before the tax is included? _____

6. The class trip is going to cost each of the fifty students $130. If the tax is 5%, what is the total cost for the entire class? _____

7. Which would cost more—a pair of earrings priced at $28 with a 7% tax or a set of posters at $29 with a 5 1/2% tax? _____

8. Your family would like to purchase the television set advertised for $458. If the tax is 7.5%, what is the total cost of the television set? _____

9. If the federal government taxes the earnings of its workers at the rate of 28%, how much tax will a worker be taxed if she earns $37,500 this year? _____

10. If two workers earn $30,000 and $45,000, respectively, what is the difference in the amount of tax each owes if each is taxed at the rate of 30%? _____

Use this space for scrap work.

115. THE MISSING LINKS

In each problem at least one space is missing a number. Fill in the missing number (or numbers) in each space to make each problem complete.

1.
```
  43
+2□
 66
```

2.
```
  138
+1□7
  275
```

3.
```
   762
+ □□5
  1177
```

4.
```
  □□5
+187
  942
```

5.
```
   56
 ×□8
 1008
```

6.
```
   3□
× 12
  408
```

7.
```
   25
×□□
  225
```

8.
```
  .92
×□.□
.736
```

9.
```
  601
-□□6
  175
```

10.
```
  6□3
-□89
  254
```

11.
```
  145
-1□9
  □6
```

12.
```
  □2□
-347
  282
```

116. A CAPITAL EXPERIENCE

Each answer to a problem found in column A has a matching answer in column B. Match the answers to the problems in columns A and B by writing the correct letters from column B in the spaces under column A. If you have correctly answered the problems, you will be able to make sense out of this activity's title. The first one is done for you.

COLUMN A

1. __a__   987

2. _____   8 squared

3. _____   the square root of 9

4. _____   .42857

5. _____ $48 \times 20 \times 6$

6. _____   6.684

7. _____   .4444

8. _____   12 cubed

9. _____   45 squared

10. _____ 16×12

11. _____ $21/22$

COLUMN B

a. 7×141

d. $4/9$

e. 24×8

i. 24×240

n. 1.671×4

o.   6912 divided by 4

r.   .9545

s. $81/27$

t. $3/7$

u.   4 cubed

v. $6075/3$

Use this space for your scrap work.

II7. MATH MATCH-UP

Here are twenty math problems that cover a number of different math areas. Do the necessary computation and then write the correct letter from column B next to the corresponding number in column A. The first one is done for you.

COLUMN A

1. __J__ 27×3 inches

2. ____ 3.14159

3. ____ 17X

4. ____ 42/2

5. ____ 360

6. ____ 9

7. ____ 7.9372

8. ____ $9\sqrt{3}$

9. ____ 73

10. ____ 12 × 5

11. ____ 200 – 4

12. ____ 2

13. ____ 18

14. ____ 4

15. ____ $2^2 \times 5$

16. ____ 36 π inches

17. ____ $2\sqrt{7}$

18. ____ 5

19. ____ 1

20. ____ 24

COLUMN B

A. -7×-3

B. $3\sqrt{125}$

C. a circle's radius if the diameter is 8

D. area of a triangle with b = 6 and h = 6

E. $4\sqrt{3} + \sqrt{75}$

F. $\sqrt{63}$

G. # of years in a score

H. Solve for ×: 3× – 14 = 13

I. pi

J. area of a square with side of 9 inches

K. solve for ×: $3X^2 – 12 = 0$

L. 14^2

M. $8^2 + 3^2$

N. $\sqrt{28}$

O. $-3 + 4$

P. # of degrees in each angle of an equilateral triangle

Q. solve for ×: 2/6 = 8/×

R. = of degrees in a circle

S. 3X + 5X + 9X

T. area of a circle with a radius of 6 inches

Name _____ Date _____ Period _____

II8. ALIVE WITH FORTY-FIVE!

Here are ten problems that require some heavy-duty thinking. Calculators are permitted (as long as your teacher approves!). Assuming your answers are all correct, when you add up all of the first digits in each answer (you should have 10 numbers), their sum should be 45.

1. John's house is 1.2 miles from the Teen Recreation Center. Kim's house is 4.5 times that distance. How far from the Teen Recreation Center is Kim's house? _____

2. A one-digit number is squared. The result is a two-digit number. When the square's digits are reversed, the number is 18 less than the two-digit square. What is the original single-digit number? _____

3. A dentist consistently earns $1300 each week throughout one year. If she is taxed at 36%, how much will she owe? _____

4. The local athletic footwear store has guaranteed a 15% discount on any item sold in the store. If your total is $102, including the discount, what was the price before the discount? _____

5. The town library has purchased, $4,230 in new books. If this is 30% of the library's total budget, how much more money does the library have in its budget? _____

6. The Allers family made $50,000 this year. If the cost of living increases 3% in each of the next 3 years, what will the family have to make during that 3rd year in order to live as they did this year? (Round off to the nearest dollar.) _____

7. If the county debt increases at the rate of $1 per minute, by how much will it increase in a 30-day period? _____

8. Linda's height has increased by 180% over the last 5 years. If she is now 62 inches, how tall was she 5 years ago? (Round off to the nearest inch.) _____

9. If Hank paid $28.20 for 20 notebooks, how much will 3 notebooks cost? _____

10. The recent fruit sale earned your school $147 this year. If this was 7% of the money collected during the sale, what was the total amount collected? _____

Use this space for your scrap work.

119. THE ANSWER BOXES

The answers to the problems below are found in these boxes. Only eight of these answers will be used. Select the correct answer from the boxes and write it in the space after the question.

4	6	9	14	57	59	81	Bob	Fran	Jill
163	176	270	308	2120	2700	3428	3600	4000	

1. If Jerry weighs 200 pounds and loses 3 pounds each week for the next 8 weeks, what will his weight be then? _____

2. Maureen can run a quarter of a mile in 90 seconds. If her speed remains consistent, how many minutes will it take Maureen to run a mile? _____ minutes

3. In their town recycling project, the students in Fairton Middle School collected 50 bottles the first day and continued to collect bottles for the next 29 days. If they collected a total of 1,770 bottles, what was their daily average? _____ bottles

4. During the first day at the Manley Audio Store, 80 CD's were sold. If sales increased by 50% for each of the next 3 days, what was the number of CD's sold on the 4th day? _____ CD's

5. Ms. Herman has 26 students in her English class. If the total number of points accumulated by the entire class on the most recent exam is 2,106 points, what was the class average? _____ %

6. Tom's baseball card collection is presently worth $2,500. He has been told that the collection's value will increase by 20% in the next year and then another 20% in the year after that. What will the collection's worth be at that time? _____ dollars

7. If Bob's chances of winning a contest are 2 out of 7, Jill's chances are 4 out of 9, and Fran's chances are 7 out of 11, who has the best chances of winning? _____

8. The 10th-grade class treasury needs to reach $1,000 by the end of the month. The treasury is currently $650. With 25 days left until the month's end, how much does the class need to average each day in order to reach the $1,000 mark? _____ dollars

Name _____ Date _____ Period _____

120. IT'S STOPWATCH TIME!

Here are ten problems that involve timing. All the answers to the problems are found in the columns below. Write the correct answer in the space provided.

42 minutes	9 1/3 hours	1.5 minutes	60 minutes	76 seconds
5 1/3 hours	221 seconds	52 minutes	5 minutes	21 seconds

1. If Jose's average quarter-mile pace is 75 seconds, what would be his mile time (in minutes)? _____

2. Marisa can run from home plate to first base in 5.25 seconds. If she runs that pace, how long will it take her to reach home plate? _____

3. Sandy can run to the top of the hill in 3.8 minutes. Paul can run the same distance in 1/3 Sandy's time. How many seconds will it take Paul to get to the top of the hill? _____

4. It takes Roberto 39 seconds to fill 3 bags of groceries. How long will it take him to fill 17 bags of groceries? _____

5. Frankie can paint 5 signs in 3.5 hours. What is the average number of minutes it takes him to paint 1 sign? _____

6. On each of the 5 school days this week, it took Jill 32 minutes to walk to school and 32 minutes to walk home from school. How many hours of walking did she do this week? _____

7. Each day Kenny's subway ride took him 33 minutes to get to his after-school job and 37 minutes to get home from the job. If he worked 8 consecutive days, how many hours did he spend on the subway? _____

8. George can do his paper route in 1.5 hours each day. With his brother helping him, he can do it in 2/3 the time. How many minutes will it take for George and his brother to do the route? _____

9. The school officials plan to increase each of the 40 minute classes by 30%. What will be the new length of each class? _____

10. The school photographer can photograph 400 students in 10 hours. How much time does she average to take each student's picture? _____

Name _____ Date _____ Period _____

121. MATH AND THE MOVIES

After you have solved each problem, write the answer *after* the problem and the code letter associated with the answer in the space provided *in front of* the problem. If you have done this correctly, you will spell out the names of three box-office smashes.

CODE LETTERS:

A=1 B=2 C=3 D=4 E=5 F=6 G=7 H=8 I=9 J=10
K=11 L=12 M=13 N=14 O=15 P=16 Q=17 R=18 S=19
T=20 U=21 V=22 W=23 X=24 Y=25 Z=26

MOVIE NO. 1

____ The number of U.S. states minus 30 _____

____ The number in a quartet plus 2 squared _____

____ The number of events in a pentathlon _____

____ The number of days in a fortnight plus 5 _____

____ 1/4 of the minutes in an hour _____

____ Its roman numeral equivalent is XXI _____

____ The number of lines in a sonnet _____

____ 1/3 of the number of days of Christmas _____

____ Its square is 225 _____

____ It's the number of people in 2 trios _____

____ Very few buildings have this floor number _____

____ 9 + 6 + 3 + 3 _____

____ One less than a score _____

____ 3 squared _____

____ 1/27 of 81 _____

MOVIE NO. 2

____ An even dozen _____

____ The number of Great Lakes _____

____ 4% of 500 _____

____ The number in an octet _____

____ The difference between a triad and a duo _____

____ The number of sides on a dodecagon _____

____ Its square root is 4.79583 _____

____ The number in the hundreds' column in 6,543 _____

____ The number of audible letters in the word queue _____

____ A baker's dozen plus three _____

156

_____ 5 less than a score _____

_____ Half of the days in February in a nonleap year _____

MOVIE NO. 3

_____ It's 3/7 of 42 _____

_____ Its cube is 3,375 _____

_____ This number times 3.75 is 11.25 _____

_____ When squared, cubed, and quadrupled, its results are all palindromes _____

_____ The next perfect square after 16 _____

122. THE PROBABILITY IS. . .

Here are some problems dealing with probability. If you have answered the problems correctly, you will have spelled out a name associated with mathematics. Write the correct letters in the spaces provided.

1. ____ The probability of selecting an ace from a standard deck of playing cards is (a) 1/13 (b) 3/26 (c) 4/13.

2. ____ The probability of selecting a diamond from a standard deck of playing cards is (q) 1/6 (r) 1/4 (s) 2/13.

3. ____ The probability of selecting the three of clubs from a standard deck of playing cards is (a) 9/52 (b) 1/13 (c) 1/52.

4. ____ A container has 4 black, 8 yellow, and 6 red balls. One of the balls is selected randomly. The probability that the ball is a black one is (f) 1/3 (g) 4/9 (h) 2/9.

5. ____ The probability of selecting a yellow ball from that same container in question 4 is (g) 5/9 (h) 2/3 (i) 4/9.

6. ____ A standard cube (die) with numbers 1, 2, 3, 4, 5, and 6 on its sides is rolled. What is the probability of rolling a 2? (m) 1/6 (n) 2/3 (o) 1/3

7. ____ If that same cube in question 6 is rolled, what is the probability of rolling an odd number? (d) 1/3 (e) 1/2 (f) 3/4

8. ____ A bat bag has 6 wooden bats and 3 aluminum bats. If two bats are taken out at random, what is the probability that both are wooden? (b) 1/6 (c) 1/2 (d) 5/12

9. ____ Using the same bag as in question 8, what is the probability that both bats are aluminum? (d) 1/8 (e) 1/12 (f) 2/9

10. ____ The probability of selecting the ace of clubs from a standard deck of playing cards is (s) 1/52 (t) 1/13 (u) 1/6.

Name _____ Date _____ Period _____

123. HARDER PROBABILITY

Here are some probability problems that will give you a run for your money. In fact, with each correct answer, you will earn a certain dollar amount in this make-believe money game. Insert the dollar amounts you earned in the spaces provided before each question's number. Add up your dollar amounts to see how well you did. Circle the correct answers. Good luck!

Each of the following five questions is worth $5. You can earn up to $25.

____ 1. A letter is selected randomly from the first thirteen letters of the alphabet. What are the chances that it is **not** a vowel? (a) 3/13 (b) 10/13 (c) 3/26

____ 2. A class consists of 13 boys and 19 girls. If a student is selected at random, what are the chances that the student is a girl? (a) 13/32 (b) 19/32 (c) 3/16

____ 3. In two tosses of the same penny, what are the chances that they will both be heads? (a) 1/8 (b) 1/2 (c) 1/4

____ 4. In two tosses of the same penny, what are the chances that you will get a combination of one head and one tail? (a) 2 out of 4 (b) 3 out of 4 (c) 1 out of 8

____ 5. In three tosses of the same penny, what are the chances of getting three tails? (a) 1 out of 4 (b) 1 out of 8 (c) 1 out of 3

Each of the following questions is worth $10. The highest you can earn in this section is $50.

____ 6. If you roll two dice, your chances of getting a total of 2 are (a) 1 in 18 (b) 1 in 8 (c) 1 in 36.

____ 7. If you roll two dice, your chances of getting a total of 7 are (a) 1 in 6 (b) 2 in 9 (c) 1 in 12.

____ 8. If you roll two dice, your chances of getting a total of 8 are (a) 5 in 36 (b) 1 in 4 (c) 1 in 36.

____ 9. If you roll two dice, your chances of getting a total of 3 are (a) 1 in 18 (b) 1 in 36 (c) 1 in 4.

____ 10. If you roll two dice, what are your chances of getting 2 fours? (a) 1 in 12 (b) 1 in 18 (c) 1 in 36.

(Hint: If you have answered all these questions correctly, the letter a *will have appeared 4 times and the other two letters,* b *and* c, *each will have appeared 3 times.)*

The amount of money you earned in this game is $ _____ .

124. FIGURING OUT THE AGES AND NUMBERS

These eight problems will introduce you to members of both my immediate and extended families. My pets are also here. Write the answers to these problems in the appropriate spaces.

1. _____ I have 2 sisters. The product of their ages is 32. The sum of their ages is 12. One sister is twice the age of the other. How old is my younger sister?

2. _____ I have three cousins on my dad's side. The product of their ages is 84. Next year the youngest will be 1/4 the age of the middle cousin. In 2 years from now, the oldest will be twice the current age of the middle. What is the age of my oldest cousin?

3. _____ What is the age of my mom if: (a) my dad is 6 years older than my mom and (b) my mom is 831/3% of my father's age and (c) 6 years ago my mom's age was 80% of my dad's age?

4. _____ How old is my older brother Joe if (a) Joe is 2 years my senior and Tom is 2 years my junior and (b) our ages add up to 42 and (c) 2 times Tom's age is 50% of 3 times Joe's age?

5. _____ How old is the youngest cousin on my mother's side if (a) the youngest is 1/3 the oldest and (b) the middle one is 2 times the youngest and (c) the middle one is 2/3 the age of the oldest and (d) in 3 years their combined ages will be 45?

6. _____ I have next door neighbors named Ralph and Jim. Ralph is twice Jim's age. In 7 years Jim will be 2/3 Ralph's age. Their current combined ages add up to 21. How old is Ralph?

7. _____ I own ducks and dogs. The number of ducks is 4 times the number of dogs. The total number of legs the ducks and dogs possess is 36. How many ducks do I own?

8. _____ I also have cats and canaries. The number of canaries is somewhere between 3 and 4 times the number of cats. There is a total of 44 legs. If 2 cats and 3 canaries were given away to friends of mine, there would only be a total of 30 legs. How many cats do I currently own?

125. PENNIES FOR YOUR THOUGHTS

A fourth grade class collected 1,225,000 pennies to help start an aquarium in their town. Their feat has inspired a number of questions about the pennies. Surely, you'll find the answers amazing. Write your responses in the appropriate spaces.

1. _____ Which would be taller? (a) the 1,225,000 pennies stacked one upon the other or (b) the Twin Towers of the World Trade Center stacked one upon the other.

2. _____ How many dollars is 1,225,000 pennies?

3. _____ Which weighs more? (a) the 1,225,000 pennies or (b) 24 players of average weight from the National Basketball Association?

4. _____ Which weighs more? (a) the 1,225,000 pennies or (b) the 11 offensive plus the 11 defensive players on your local high school football team.

5. _____ If the pennies were placed side to side, they would cover approximately what distance? (a) 14.5 miles (b) 200 football fields (c) 2 miles.

6. _____ How many quarters are the equivalent of 1,225,000 pennies?

7. _____ If it takes exactly 1 second to count each penny, approximately how long will it take to count the 1,225,000 pennies? (a) 2 days (b) 8 days (c) 14 days.

8. _____ A football field is 100 yards. Approximately how many football fields will the 1,225,000 pennies cover? (a) 25 (b) 255 (c) 2555.

9. _____ A marathon course is 26.2 miles. What approximate percent of the course will the 1,225,000 pennies cover? (a) 23% (b) 53% (c) 73%.

10. _____ The pennies weigh approximately 6,800 pounds. Your family car weighs 2,725 pounds. What percent of the pennies' weight is your car's weight?

Section Six

THE WORLD AROUND YOU

126. LIGHTS! CAMERA! ACTION!

Here's your chance to see how the professionals do it as you look at film-making from behind the camera and without the glitz. Select one of your favorite books and answer these questions making believe the book will be made into a made-for-television movie. It's a wrap!

1. Your book's title: _____

2. Author: _____

3. Setting: _____

4. Who are the book's main characters? What current movie stars will play these roles on screen? List them here. Give reasons why you have selected these movie stars for these parts. _____
   _____
   _____

5. Would you add or delete any of the book's characters? Why or why not? _____
   _____

6. Will you add or delete any of the book's scenes? Why or why not?_____
   _____

7. Who is your intended viewing audience?_____

8. What three scenes from the book will you show on commercials advertising the movie? Why would you select these scenes?

   Scene 1: _____
   _____

   Scene 2: _____
   _____

   Scene 3: _____
   _____

9. During which viewing hours do you intend to air these commercials? Why? _____
   _____

10. What specific products will you use for your commercials? Why? _____
    _____
    _____

11. Are there any major changes you will make in the plot or other aspects of the movie?
    _____
    _____

12. What problems do you expect when adapting this book into a movie? _____
    _____
    _____

127. A DAY AT THE BEACH

Some interesting situations occurred the day that Dan and Gary, two ninth graders, went to the beach. Write what you feel they should have done in each situation as you consider all of the possible repercussions to their actions. Then discuss your opinions with your classmates.

1. Prices at the state beach are considered by many to be rather expensive. A hot dog is $2.50, a can of ice tea is $2.00, and an ice cream bar is $3.25. Illegal vendors who walk the beach sell these same items at half the cost. Should the two boys buy from these illegal vendors? _____

_____

_____

2. Dan and Gary have their blankets far away from the lifeguard stand at the beach where the playing of radios is prohibited. A group of eighteen-year-olds is blasting annoying music from their huge radios. What should Dan and Gary do? _____

_____

_____

3. The boys find a wallet with $75 and no identification inside it. What should they do?

_____

_____

4. The boys see two muscular guys in their early twenties steal food and money from the unoccupied blanket next to them. What should Dan and Gary do? _____

_____

_____

5. On a hot and crowded evening at the beach, Dan and Gary see a five-year-old boy who appears to be lost. He is crying and nobody else seems to pay attention to him. The lifeguards and beach security have gone home for the evening. What should they do?

_____

_____

128. A MESSAGE IN A BOTTLE

Imagine that you are walking along the seashore and you find a bottle with the following message written inside: "I have made friends with the White Rabbit and the Cheshire Cat." The message would have been from Alice, the title character in *Alice in Wonderland* by Lewis Carroll.

Using literary characters, historical figures, movie actors and actresses, television characters, friends, or anyone else you wish as message senders, create clever messages that these people might have written. Write your messages in the spaces provided.

_____
_____
_____
_____
_____
_____
_____
_____
_____
_____
_____
_____
_____
_____
_____
_____
_____
_____
_____

129. HOW DOES IT MOVE?

In the space provided, tell whether each of the following means of transportation primarily flies, floats, or rolls.

1. plane _____

2. submarine _____

3. jet ski _____

4. kayak _____

5. bicycle _____

6. train _____

7. ocean liner _____

8. steamship _____

9. jet _____

10. caravel _____

11. raft _____

12. truck _____

13. lorry _____

14. subway _____

15. moped _____

16. helicopter _____

17. go-cart _____

18. rocket _____

19. blimp _____

20. pontoon _____

21. tricycle _____

22. Italian gondola _____

23. automobile _____

24. canoe _____

25. hot-air balloon _____

26. hot rod _____

27. catamaran _____

28. dirigible _____

29. caboose _____

30. unicycle _____

31. zeppelin _____

32. motorcycle _____

33. skateboard _____

34. bus _____

35. locomotive _____

130. THE WORLD OF WORK

What are some jobs that were not around twenty-five years ago? What are the jobs of the future, those that will come into existence in the next twenty-five years? List those jobs in their proper columns and give reasons why they were created or will need to be created. An example of each is done for you.

JOBS THAT WHERE NOT HERE TWENTY-FIVE YEARS AGO

1. AIDS researcher _____   Since the inception of AIDS in the early 1980s, scientists have tried to
find its cause and stop its spread _____
_____

2. _____   _____
_____
_____

3. _____   _____
_____
_____

4. _____   _____
_____
_____

5. _____   _____
_____
_____

JOBS OF THE FUTURE

1. Robotics specialist _____   Since people are so busy in their work and other activities, robots will
be taking over more of the people's responsibilities. Robots will also be needed in the workplace. _____
_____

2. _____   _____
_____
_____

3. _____   _____
_____
_____

4. _____   _____

_____

_____

5. _____   _____

_____

_____

JOBS THAT MIGHT BE ELIMINATED IN TEN YEARS

1. _____   _____

_____

_____

2. _____   _____

_____

_____

3. _____   _____

_____

_____

Name _____ Date _____ Period _____

131. NEWSPAPERS AND THEIR SECTIONS

Here are sixteen sections found in many newspapers. Describe the subject matter of each section. When possible or necessary, give an example to reinforce your statements. Compare your answers with those of your classmates.

1. ADVICE COLUMNS: _____

2. BOOK REVIEWS: _____

3. BRIDGE: _____

4. CLASSIFIEDS: _____

5. COMICS: _____

6. PUZZLES: _____

7. EDITORIALS: _____

8. HEALTH AND FITNESS: _____

9. HOROSCOPES: _____

10. OBITUARIES: _____

11. TELEVISION LISTINGS: _____

12. SPORTS: _____

13. MOVIE LISTINGS: _____

14. WEATHER: _____

15. BUSINESS: _____

16. NEWS: (a) Local (b) National (c) International _____

171

132. COUNTRIES, CAPITALS, AND CURRENCIES

Twenty countries are listed in column A. Column B features scrambled spellings of the countries' capital cities. Column C lists their primary monetary units, also scrambled. Unscramble the capital cities and their monetary units in the spaces provided after each column. *(Hint! The real word begins with the first letter of the scrambled word.)*

COLUMN A	COLUMN B	COLUMN C
1. Australia	Cneraarb _____	dlaolr _____
2. Austria	Veiann _____	shligcnli_____
3. Brazil	Bsairila _____	ucrzieor _____
4. Canada	Otawta_____	dlaorl _____
5. China	Bengiji _____	ynau_____
6. France	Prasi_____	facnr_____
7. Germany	Blirne _____	mrak _____
8. Greece	Anseht _____	damcahr _____
9. India	Nwe Dlihe_____	reepu _____
10. Ireland	Dbnilu _____	pdnuo_____
11. Israel	Jmelasuer _____	seelhk _____
12. Italy	Rmeo _____	lria _____
13. Japan	Tykoo _____	yne _____
14. Mexico	Mxecio Ctyi_____	pose _____
15. Norway	Ools_____	kenro _____
16. Poland	Waaswr _____	zoylt_____
17. Spain	Mdardi_____	peesat _____
18. Sweden	Skmlothco _____	kanor _____
19. Switzerland	Bner _____	facrn_____
20. Turkey	Aaarkn_____	lair _____

133. RATE THE INVENTIONS

What are the greatest inventions and discoveries of all time? How can one invention be valued more than another? By what criteria are you making the decision about the invention's or discovery's worth? For each pair, circle the one that you feel is more beneficial for the world. In the space provided, give reasons why you feel one is better than the other.

1. automobiles versus trains _____

2. computer versus laser disc _____

3. radio versus television _____

4. eyeglasses versus hearing aids _____

5. telephone versus mail _____

6. elevator versus subway _____

7. heart transplant versus lung transplant _____

8. air conditioning versus heat _____

9. jets versus high-speed trains _____

10. microwave oven versus dishwasher _____

11. radar versus satellite dishes _____

12. vitamins versus respirator to prolong life _____

13. penicillin versus morphine _____

14. dentures versus wigs _____

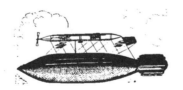

134. ALL ROADS LEAD TO SOME CONFUSION

Here is an interesting activity that deals with different types of roads and their names.
Describe the type of road. Is it long, wide, secluded, heavily traveled? How is it different
from the others? Think of roads in your town or city that have these names. Compare your
answers with those of your classmates.

1. Lane: _____

2. Court: _____

3. Drive: _____

4. Avenue: _____

5. Highway: _____

6. Parkway: _____

7. Boulevard: _____

8. Place: _____

9. Street: _____

10. Road: _____

Name _____ Date _____ Period _____

135. THE NEEDED PRODUCT

Are you another Ben Franklin, Thomas Jefferson, or Thomas Edison? They were great inventors. You might be too! Here is your opportunity to introduce that product that the world could certainly use. Answer the following questions that deal with your invention and compare your product with those of your classmates.

1. What is your product? _____

2. What need does your product serve? _____
   _____

3. How will your product be different from other similar products currently on the market? _____
   _____

4. How do you plan to field test this product? _____
   _____

5. Is your product created for a specific age group? If so, what ages? _____

6. What are some of the key points you will make in advertising this product? _____
   _____

7. Where will you primarily advertise this product? Television, radio, newspapers, magazines, billboards? _____
   _____

8. What are some of the key phrases you will use in your advertising campaign? _____
   _____

9. In what type of stores will the public be able to find this product? _____
   _____

10. Approximately how much will you charge for this product? _____

136. STORING THE NAMES

A walk through the main part of town can be an interesting way to learn about different occupations. The names below are store signs that you might have noticed as you walked through town last Saturday. Some of them may have been new to you, while others probably seemed more familiar. In the space provided, write the type of work each of these occupations entails.

1. Accountant: _____

2. Architect: _____

3. Attorneys: _____

4. Boat Transporter: _____

5. Building Restorers: _____

6. Career Counselor: _____

7. Caterers: _____

8. Chiropractor: _____

9. Pediatric Dentist: _____

10. Excavating Contractors: _____

11. Fork-Lift Operators: _____

12. Gutter and Downspout Installers: _____

13. Importers: _____

14. Investment Consultants: _____

15. Landscape Architects: _____

16. Locksmith: _____

17. Mason: _____

18. Meteorological Consultants: _____

19. Mortgage Experts: _____

20. Notaries Public: _____

Copyright © 1996 by John Wiley & Sons, Inc.

Name _____ Date _____ Period _____

137. WHAT DO I DO?

These were storefront signs Ben saw as he walked through town. He has some idea what some of them mean, but he is stumped by others. Help Ben to know more about these jobs by explaining the type of work that each does.

1. Opticians: _____

2. Orthodontist: _____

3. Pawnbrokers: _____

4. Pest Controllers: _____

5. Pet Groomers: _____

6. Pharmacist: _____

7. Physical Therapist: _____

8. Physician: _____

9. Plastic Surgeon: _____

10. Podiatrist: _____

11. Rubbish Removers: _____

12. Stationers: _____

13. Stockbrokers: _____

14. Surveyors: _____

15. Taxidermist: _____

16. Transmission Experts: _____

17. Vertical Blind Installers and Cleaners: _____

18. Veterinarian: _____

19. Wheel Aligners: _____

20. Woodworkers: _____

138. BEING SENSITIVE TO YOUR SURROUNDINGS

Your five senses help you to describe such diverse places as a gymnasium, a cafeteria, and a train station. Using your five senses of sight, smell, sound, taste, and touch, describe what you might possibly see, smell, hear, taste, and touch at the following places. Give at least five sensory describers per location using adjectives whenever possible. The first one is done for you.

1. a beach:
   see: crashing waves, surfers, gray sand
   smell: saltwater, suntan lotion
   hear: roaring ocean, children playing, radios
   taste: hot dogs, hamburgers, iced tea
   touch: grains of hot sand, cool ocean water

2. baseball stadium:
   see: _____
   smell: _____
   hear: _____
   taste: _____
   touch: _____

3. an amusement park:
   see: _____
   smell: _____
   hear: _____
   taste: _____
   touch: _____

4. a city park:
   see: _____
   smell: _____
   hear: _____
   taste: _____
   touch: _____

5. a hospital:
   see: _____
   smell: _____
   hear: _____
   taste: _____
   touch: _____

6. a city street at rush hour:

see: _____

smell: _____

hear: _____

taste: _____

touch: _____

7. your school cafeteria:

see: _____

smell: _____

hear: _____

taste: _____

touch: _____

Now list two other locations and what you would see, smell, hear, taste, and touch.

8. _____:

see: _____

smell: _____

hear: _____

taste: _____

touch: _____

9. _____:

see: _____

smell: _____

hear: _____

taste: _____

touch: _____

139. MIXED-UP PROVERBS

Fifteen proverbs have been split in half. Match the first part of the proverb with its second part by writing the corresponding number next to the second part of the proverb. The first one is done for you.

FIRST PARTS

1. All that glitters . . .
2. Live and . . .
3. Practice makes . . .
4. Where there's a will . . .
5. From little acorns . . .
6. A stitch in time . . .
7. Don't count your chickens . . .
8. Nothing ventured . . .
9. Two wrongs . . .
10. Every cloud . . .
11. Out of sight . . .
12. Honesty . . .
13. Many hands . . .
14. You can't have your cake . . .
15. Better late . . .

SECOND PART

__1__ is not gold.

____ make light work.

____ perfect.

____ has a silver lining.

____ saves nine.

____ nothing gained.

____ don't make a right.

____ before they hatch.

____ there's a way.

____ than never.

____ let live.

____ big oaks grow.

____ is the best policy.

____ out of mind.

____ and eat it too.

Now discuss the meanings of these proverbs with your classmates.

140. BEING OBSERVANT

Are you aware of things around you? Here is your chance to compare your observations with those of your classmates. A scene is given and you are asked to record some of the people and things that are or were present at this place or occasion. Write your responses in the appropriate spaces.

A Graduation Ceremony: crowds of people, mortarboards, tassels, speeches, processions, tears, laughter, cameras, relatives, songs . . .

1. A day at the beach: _____

_____

2. A school examination: _____

_____

3. A "sweet sixteen" party: _____

_____

4. The school cafeteria after lunch: _____

_____

5. A professional sporting event: _____

_____

6. A wedding ceremony: _____

_____

7. Woodstock: _____

_____

8. A music concert at a stadium or similar location: _____

_____

_____

141. INITIALS CAN TELL MUCH

Michael Jordan's initials are perfect for this activity since M. J. can also stand for Mighty Jumper. Using a person's initials, create words that describe the person accurately. A few examples have been given to get you in the proper mind-set for the game. Good luck!

H. A.	Hank Aaaron	Homer Ace
T. E.	Thomas Edison	Talent Extraordinaire
L. I.	Lee Iacocca	Leading Industrialist
A. L.	Abraham Lincoln	Admired Liberator
E. P.	Elvis Presley	Exciting Performer

Name _____ Date _____ Period _____

142. I WISH I COULD HAVE BEEN THERE...

Here's your chance to go back in history. In each instance circle the event you'd like to have witnessed and, in the space provided, write why you have selected that event.

1. The destruction of the Berlin Wall or Neil Armstrong's walk on the moon? _____

_____

2. Hank Aaron's 715th home run or America's hockey victory over Russia in the 1980s Olympics? _____

_____

3. The signing of the Declaration of Independence or the signing of the Treaty of Versailles? _____

_____

4. The first heart transplant operation or the birth of the Dionne quintuplets? _____

_____

5. 1969 Woodstock or 1994 Woodstock? _____

_____

6. Working in the lab with Thomas Edison or recording a record with Michael Jackson?

_____

7. Aboard ship with Christopher Columbus or flying with Chuck Yeager? _____

_____

8. A British king's coronation or an American president's inauguration?_____

_____

9. Sandra Day O'Connor's swearing in as a Supreme Court Justice or a peace march led by Martin Luther King, Jr.? _____

_____

10. In an Indy 500 race car on Memorial Day or in a movie starring Sylvester Stallone?

_____

_____

143. MIXED-UP MOVIE TITLES

Movie theater employee Monty has a problem. He was asked to list some memorable movies on the theater wall where theater-goers could easily see the titles. It is now one hour before the door is to open and he has words all over the place. Your help is desperately needed! Cross out the words you use and then write the correct title in the spaces provided. All the words will be used.

and—Apollo—Back—Back—Batman—Beast—Beauty—Beverly—Bridges—Cop— County—Dead—Empire—Forever—Forrest—Framed—Free—Future—Gump—Hills— Honey—I—Indiana—Jedi—Jones—Jurassic—Kids—King—Lethal—Lion—Madison— Music—of—of—of—Park—Poets—Rabbit—Return—Roger—Shrunk—Society—Sound— Star—Star—Strikes—The—The—The—The—the—the—the—the—13—to—Trek— Wars—Weapon—Who—Willy

Name _____ Date _____ Period _____

144. REVIEWING THE MOVIES

Here is your chance to have your say regarding movies. Write your responses about movies' purposes in the space provided. If time permits, discuss your answers with your classmates.

1. What purposes do movies serve? _____
_____

2. Are you in favor of the movie ratings such as R, PG, NC–17, and PG–13? Why? ____
_____

3. What movie is you favorite? Why? _____
_____

4. What movie scene scared you? Why? _____
_____
_____

5. What movie was inspirational for you? Why? _____
_____
_____

6. What movie depicts teenagers in a favorable way? _____
_____

7. What movie depicts teenagers in an unfavorable way? _____
_____

8. Categorize the various types of movies, such as adventure, comedy, and so forth. ___
_____

9. What type of movies seem to do well at the box office? Why? _____
_____

10. What movie taught you more about a different culture? _____
_____

11. What movie scene seemed hard to shoot? Why? _____
_____
_____

12. What character, in what movie, can you relate to? _____
_____
_____

13. If you could make a movie, what would be its subject matter? Why have you chosen this area? _____
_____
_____

145. BUYING A CAR

Before you know it, you might be purchasing a car. Knowing the car lingo is as important as having enough money to buy the car. Translate the "car language" used in the following ads by writing the complete ad in the space provided.

Ad 1: Ford 92 Crown Victoria, all pwr, lo mi, warr, mint

_____

Ad 2: Merc 93, 4 dr, auto, a/c, 32K

_____

Ad 3: Honda Prelude, a/t, red, 5 spd, lthr, neg. price

_____

Ad 4: Plymouth 91, new tir, ps/pb/ac

_____

Ad 5: Camaro 89, auto, lo mi, p/w, excel cond

_____

Ad 6: Eagle 90, new trans, 70K mi, wht ext, warr

_____

Ad 7: Chevy 88, Beretta, excel in & out, wht wl tir, ask 3500

_____

Ad 8: Corvette 75, 4 spd, org own, new eng, alrm, neg

_____

Ad 9: Chevy Van 88, V8, new trans, am/fm cass, loaded

_____

Ad 10: Buick 83 Regal, 8 cyl, nds brks, dl exhst, 77K mi

_____

146. CONNIE'S CONFUSING CALENDAR

Connie is so busy at her job that she sometimes feels as though she doesn't know what day it is. Help Connie straighten out her calendar by writing the correct month next to these American holidays. Though all of the months are **not** used, a month may be used more than once.

1. _____ Lincoln's Birthday
2. _____ Independence Day
3. _____ Labor Day
4. _____ Mother's Day
5. _____ Memorial Day
6. _____ Groundhog Day
7. _____ Father's Day
8. _____ Columbus Day
9. _____ Halloween
10. _____ Thanksgiving
11. _____ Election Day
12. _____ Martin Luther King, Jr. Day
13. _____ Flag Day
14. _____ New Year's Day
15. _____ Washington's Birthday
16. _____ Veterans Day

147. THE WORLD OF WORK

It's time for an opinion poll! This poll needs to know why you feel the way you do about certain occupations. Answer these questions by circling your choices. Be prepared to support your choice with facts and reasonable opinions.

Who should be paid more?

1. a doctor or a lawyer?

2. a teacher or an airplane pilot?

3. a baseball player or a dentist?

4. a nurse or a model?

5. an opera singer or an Indy 500 driver?

6. a mayor or a talk-show host?

7. a postal carrier or a truck driver?

8. a football coach or a veterinarian?

9. a barber or a tattoo artist?

10. a plumber or a cartoonist?

11. a magician or a comedian?

12. a scientist or a poet?

13. a make-up artist or a stunt man?

14. a policeman or a fireman?

15. a Broadway actor or a Hollywood movie actor?

16. a brain surgeon or a cardiologist?

17. a television anchorperson or a major city's newspaper editor?

18. a tree surgeon or an architect?

19. a waiter or a custodian?

20. a chef or an air-traffic controller?

148. CREATIVE LICENSE PLATES

You have become the unofficial license plate designer. Your job is to create interesting license plates for television and movie celebrities, musicians, historical figures, authors, literary figures, occupations, classmates, and friends. Restrict your license plates to no more than eight letters and/or numbers (not including necessary spaces between words or numbers).

Here are a few examples:

an intensive care unit nurse . . . ICU RN
a delicatessen owner . . . HAMNRYE
Noah from Noah's Ark . . . 2BY2BY2
Humpty Dumpty . . . FALL GUY

_____
_____
_____
_____
_____
_____
_____
_____
_____
_____
_____
_____
_____
_____
_____
_____
_____
_____
_____
_____
_____
_____
_____
_____

149. JOBS . . . JOBS . . . JOBS . . .

Selecting a job that is best for you can be a difficult job in itself! The following questions ask you to consider different employment possibilities. Some questions ask you to evaluate various jobs and their good and bad points. Answer the questions in the spaces provided, and then be ready to discuss your responses with your classmates.

1. List three jobs that are seasonal.

_____ _____ _____

2. List three dangerous jobs.

_____ _____ _____

3. List three jobs that require great intelligence.

_____ _____ _____

4. List three jobs that require quick thinking skills.

_____ _____ _____

5. List three jobs that require good physical stamina.

_____ _____ _____

6. List three jobs that require good organizational skills.

_____ _____ _____

7. List three jobs that should pay well.

_____ _____ _____

8. List three jobs that should pay more than they now do.

_____ _____ _____

9. List three jobs that should pay less than they now do.

_____ _____ _____

10. List three jobs that require the ability to get along with others.

_____ _____ _____

11. List three jobs in which one works primarily by himself or herself.

_____ _____ _____

12. List three jobs that require advanced educational training.

_____ _____ _____

13. List three jobs that should be thought of more highly by the public.

_____ _____ _____

14. List three jobs that involve patience.

_____ _____ _____

15. List three jobs that require much time away from home.

_____ _____ _____

Name _____ Date _____ Period _____

150. THE SEVEN NECESSARY OCCUPATIONS

Let's imagine for a while that the world had to start all over. Nothing exists but water, land, trees, animals, and 50 people whose ages range from 10 to 50. Trying to restart the world, your group of 50 has put you in charge of selecting the seven most necessary occupations to get the world going again. No training for any of these occupations is necessary.

    In the spaces provided, list the seven occupations and the reasons why you'd select each one. The order of selection is not based on importance.

1. _____   _____

_____

_____

2. _____   _____

_____

_____

3. _____   _____

_____

_____

4. _____   _____

_____

_____

5. _____   _____

_____

_____

6. _____   _____

_____

_____

7. _____   _____

_____

_____

151. FINDING YOUR WAY AROUND THE LIBRARY

Many libraries are organized according to the Dewey Decimal System, an invention of Melvil Dewey in 1876. Here are the ten major categories of classification. They are further broken down into subdivisions. In the space provided, write the general group in which each of the books is found. Each of the groups is used at least once.

000–009   General works . . . encyclopedias, periodicals, newspapers
100–199   Philosophy . . . esthetics, psychology, logic, ethics
200–299   Religion . . . Bible, theology, church
300–399   Social Sciences . . . sociology, economics, law, education
400–499   Language . . . dictionaries, grammars
500–599   Pure Science . . . mathematics, astronomy, physics, chemistry
600–699   Technology . . . engineering, home economics, business
700–799   The Arts . . . sculpture, drawing, painting, music
800–899   Literature . . . poems, plays
900–999   History . . . geography, travel, histories

1. _____ 50 Strange Stories of the Supernatural
2. _____ Thirty Years That Shook Physics
3. _____ Studies in Words
4. _____ History of the Land of Israel Until 1980
5. _____ Film Editing
6. _____ Hooked On Literature!
7. _____ Reality Therapy
8. _____ Solarizing Your Present Home
9. _____ Arthritis Without Aspirin
10. _____ Getting Started in Stocks
11. _____ Graphs and Their Uses
12. _____ The IQ Controversy
13. _____ Making Saints
14. _____ China's Socialist Revolution
15. _____ Death and Eternal Life
16. _____ Beginning the Chinese Language
17. _____ Christian Ethics
18. _____ Violence in America
19. _____ The Splendid Art of Opera
20. _____ Practical English Writing Skills

152. ARGUABLE TOPICS

Here are five real-life topics that are interesting topics to debate. In the space below each topic, list four supporting points of evidence for your side of the issue. Be sure your evidence is factual and not merely emotional.

1. Professional sports athletes should make several million dollars per year even though the country's president makes far less than half a million dollars per year.

(a)

(b)

(c)

(d)

2. Once a driver turns seventy years old, a driver's relicensing process, including a driver's road test, should be mandatory.

(a)

(b)

(c)

(d)

3. Certain high school subjects should not be a required part of the curriculum. If a student wishes to take the subject, he or she may elect to do so, but it should not be a requirement.

(a)

(b)

(c)

(d)

4. Should more money be spent on AIDS research or cancer research?

(a)

(b)

(c)

(d)

5. The government should control what type of programs are shown on all television stations.

(a)

(b)

(c)

(d)

153. WHAT TIME IS IT?

Days, weeks, months, years, decades, scores, centuries, and millenniums (or millennia) are terms used in measuring time. This exercise will quiz you on those terms. Write the correct letter in the space provided. If your answers are correct, two ten-letter vacation attractions will be found in the answer column.

1. _____ The number of years in six score is (A) 100 (B) 60 (C) 70 (D) 120.

2. _____ The sum of three centuries, two weeks, and three decades is how many weeks? (G) 14,502 (H) 15,632 (I) 17,162 (J) none of these.

3. _____ Which year is near the middle of the thirteenth century? (S) 1248 (T) 1348 (U) 1448 (V) 1384

4. _____ Which was the year after 1 B.C.? (L) 0 (M) 2 B.C. (N) 1 A.D. (O) none of these

5. _____ How many weeks are in six centuries? (D) 32,100 (E) 31,200 (F) 33,000 (G) none of these

6. _____ The number of weeks in two scores minus the number of years in a century leaves what remainder? (W) 560 (X) 760 (Y) 1,980 (Z) 1,000

7. _____ Which year is in the thirty-third century? (K) 3301 (L) 3201 (M) 3401 (N) none of these.

8. _____ How many decades are in five millenniums? (A) 50,000 (B) 5,000 (C) 500,000 (D) none of these

9. _____ How many months are in seven decades? (M) 480 (N) 840 (O) 4,400 (P) none of these

10. _____ Which year was included in the fourth decade of the third century? (B) 203 (C) 297 (D) both A and B (E) neither A nor B

11. _____ When you divide the number of years in eight decades by the number of weeks in two months, the answer is (L) 12 (M) 10 (N) 40 (D) 80

12. _____ When you multiply the number of weeks in a year by the number of years in three decades, the answer is (T) 1,560 (U) 1,650 (V) 640 (W) none of these

13. _____ Which year was in the twelfth century B.C.? (Q) 1237 B.C. (R) 1131 B.C. (S) 1349 B.C. (T) none of these

14. _____ Multiplying the number of days in a fortnight by the number of years in a score by the number of years in four centuries gives what answer? (S) 56,000 (T) 12,400 (U) 112,000 (V) none of these

15. _____ Which year is in the second third of the twentieth century? (R) 1925 (S) 1950 (T) 1978 (U) 2056

16. _____ Which year is in the first quarter of the first decade of the nineteenth century? (G) 2009 (H) 1801 (I) 1902 (J) none of these

17. _____ Which year is in the last fifth of the last decade of the ninth century? (M) 899 (N) 999 (O) 895 (P) none of these

18. _____ Which year is in the third decade of the seventeenth century? (N) 1737 (O) 1627 (P) 1727 (Q) 1637

19. _____ How many weeks are in fifteen fortnights? (R) 30 (S) 45 (T) 60 (U) none of these

20. _____ When you add the number of months in a year to the number of years in two score to the number of weeks in two years, the total is (D) 88 (E) 156 (F) 94 (G) 148

Section Seven

ME

Name _____ Date _____ Period _____

154. THE ME PAGE

Here are fourteen questions all dealing with you! Answer each as honestly as possible.

1. Why did your parents give you your name? Were you named after a relative, movie star, athlete? _____
_____

2. What does your first name mean? What does your last name mean? _____
_____

3. In what ways do you consider yourself special or unique? _____
_____

4. In what ways are you much like others your age? _____
_____

5. When are you happiest? _____
_____

6. When are you not happy? _____
_____

7. How are you emotionally hurt most easily? _____
_____

8. What are your favorite leisure activities? _____
_____

9. What is your favorite movie? Why? _____
_____

10. What is your favorite television program? Why? _____
_____

11. Whom do you consider your role model? Why? _____
_____

12. If you could visit any country, which would you visit? Why? _____
_____

13. What is an accomplishment you are proud of? _____
_____

14. What is an aspect about yourself that you would like to improve? _____
_____

(If it is not too personal, discuss these answers with a classmate.)

Name _____ Date _____ Period _____

155. THE TEENAGER'S PAGE

This page is devoted to you, the teenager. Here is your chance to express your thoughts about this time of your life. Answer as honestly as you can and then discuss these responses with your classmates.

1. What are some positive aspects of being a teenager?_____
   _____

2. What are some negative aspects of being a teenager? _____
   _____

3. What are some major concerns of today's teenagers? Are they much different from
   the concerns of teenagers of past generations? How? _____
   _____
   _____

4. When do teens feel most stressed? _____
   _____

5. What are the teenagers' major complaints about the world as it is today? _____
   _____

6. What is some advice you would give to the young people who will soon be teenagers?
   _____
   _____

7. What are some stereotypes associated with being a teenager? _____
   _____

8. What song is a favorite among teenagers? Why? _____
   _____

9. What are some areas of disagreement between teenagers and their parents? Why? _
   _____

10. How, if at all, will the teens of the next generation, your own children, be similar to
    or different from your generation of teens? _____
    _____

156. YOUR PERSONAL WISH LIST

Your teacher will tell you that an infinitive is the combination of the word "to" followed by the singular present form of a verb. You must respond to this activity with infinitives only. Here is your personal wish list composed of ten hopes, dreams, goals, or whatever else you would like to call them. Write your infinitives in the spaces provided. Two examples are given for you.

Examples: to get along better with my brother; to pass all my subjects

1. _____

2. _____

3. _____

4. _____

5. _____

6. _____

7. _____

8. _____

9. _____

10. _____

(If it is not too personal, compare your wish list with those of your classmates.)

Name _____ Date _____ Period _____

157. I'D PREFER...

Life is full of choices. This activity presents some interesting, hypothetical situations and then asks you to make some decisions. Circle your decision and then in the proper space, write at least one reason for your choice. Be prepared to support your choices as you and your classmates discuss these answers.

Would you rather . . .

1. be healthy or wealthy? _____
_____

2. be good-looking or athletic? _____
_____

3. lose your sight or your hearing? _____
_____

4. sing well or play an instrument well? _____
_____

5. be smart or athletic? _____
_____

6. Be a good parent or an unmarried, successful businessperson? _____
_____

7. Win a full college scholarship or tour Europe free for a year? _____
_____

8. own a sports car or have a small role on a somewhat popular television program? __
_____

9. hit a home run in the state championship game or win an award for your charity towards the elderly? _____
_____

10. be popular or be the student with the highest grade point average in your class? __
_____

Name _____ Date _____ Period _____

158. LOOKING AT LITERATURE

Your favorite book? play? character? setting? scene? These are some of the questions that might pop up in this activity. You can share some of these answers with your classmates and even stir up a debate with them. Write your answers in the spaces provided. In these questions, novels, plays, short stories, and poems are all included in the term "work." Have fun!

1. A character who reminds me of myself is _____ from the work entitled _____ because _____.

2. The character whose actions I find admirable is _____ from the work _____ because _____.

3. The work whose title is symbolic is _____ written by _____ because _____.

4. The work whose title is appropriate is _____ written by _____ because _____.

5. The author I'd most like to meet is _____ because _____
_____.

6. A character I'd like to meet is _____ because _____
_____.

7. If two characters from separate works could meet, I'd like to see _____ from the work _____ meet _____ from the work _____ because _____.

8. A work whose setting I'd like to visit is _____ written by _____ because _____
_____.

9. A scene I'd like to have been a part of is a scene from the work _____ written by _____. In this scene (tell what happens) _____
_____.

10. An animal who has an important part in the work's plot is _____ from the work _____. This animal's part is important because _____
_____.

11. A work I wish could have a sequel is _____ because _____

_____.

12. A work whose plot I found confusing is _____ written

   by _____. It was confusing because _____

_____.

Name _____ Date _____ Period _____

159. IF I WERE. . .

A man once remarked, "If I were a car, I'd be a Mercedes." When questioned, he gave several reasons why he felt he was more like a Mercedes than a Lincoln, Toyota, or Corvette. It does lead to interesting ideas and discussions. . . .

Here are some more possible situations in which you are asked to compare yourself to other people, places, and things. Think about whom or what you will select and then give good reasons why you have made that selection. If you need more space, use the reverse side of the paper.

1. If I were an animal, I'd be a(n) _____ because _____
_____.

2. If I were an automobile, I'd be a(n) _____ because _____
_____.

3. If I were a geometric figure, I'd be a(n) _____ because _____
_____.

4. If I were a professional sports team, I'd be the _____ because _____
_____.

5. If I were a major American city, I'd be _____ because _____
_____.

6. If I were a famous historical figure, I'd be _____ because _____
_____.

7. If I were a popular song, I'd be _____ because _____
_____.

8. If I were a type of food, I'd be a(n) _____ because _____
_____.

9. If I were a vacation spot, I'd be _____ because _____
_____.

10. If I were a major event in world history, I'd be _____,
    because _____
_____.

160. IN TOUCH WITH YOUR EMOTIONS

Each day we encounter different people and events that make us react in various ways. Some people make us laugh, while others annoy us. Coping with an unpleasant situation is different from experiencing a funny moment.

In the space provided, use at least three words to describe how you would feel in each of the following situations. The first one is done for you. The words used in that situation are typical: they don't necessarily have to be the same ones that you would write down.

SITUATION	EMOTIONS EXPERIENCED
1. You've lost your wallet in school:	panic, frustration, helplessness
2. You've scored the winning goal:	_____
3. Your parents have yelled at you:	_____
4. You've failed another major exam:	_____
5. You are going to eat your favorite meal:	_____
6. Your friend who had moved away surprises you with a visit:	_____
7. You are waiting in the dentist's office:	_____
8. You have been getting a busy signal for half an hour straight:	_____
9. You've ripped your expensive jeans:	_____
10. Your parents are arguing with each other:	_____
11. You've been cut from the school team:	_____
12. You are the new class president:	_____
13. You've chipped your tooth:	_____
14. You made the team and your best friend didn't:	_____
15. Your teacher calls home with positive news about your grades:	_____

Name _____ Date _____ Period _____

161. TELEVISION

Undoubtedly, television has a major impact on the lives of many people. Though some would argue, television does reflect a culture's values and beliefs, to a degree. Do you agree with this?

This activity asks you to do some thinking about this important medium. Answer as honestly as you can and then discuss your answers with your classmates. Some interesting points will surely be raised. If more room is needed for your answers, use the reverse side.

1. What is television's purpose? Does it have more than one purpose? _____
   _____

2. Approximately how many hours of television do you watch each week during the school year? _____

3. What are some types of shows you usually watch? Are they comedies, educational, informational, realistic, dramatic? _____
   _____

4. If certain shows were going to be canceled, what three shows would you least like to see taken off the air? _____
   _____

5. What purposes do the shows you listed in number 4 serve? _____
   _____

6. What are some of your complaints about television and its programs? _____
   _____

7. Are there enough shows that deal with being a teenager?_____
   _____

8. If your answer to the previous question is "No," what kinds of teenage programs would you suggest? _____
   _____

9. Why do you or why don't you usually watch the news?_____
   _____

10. Your community is preparing a time capsule which will be opened fifty years from now. Your class has been asked to select one television show that realistically reflects the current times. Which show would you select? Give reasons for your choice. _____
    _____
    _____

162. IT'S DINNER TIME

Get ready, get set, go! It's dinner time! Money is no object. The place is your choice. The food to be served is exactly what your taste buds desire.

    You are going to have dinner with four famous people. The guests you can invite can be living or dead, fictional or real. The only requirement is that the guests must be famous people. Fill in the necessary information and start right in! *Bon appétit!*

DINNER LOCATION: _____

THE MENU INCLUDES THE FOLLOWING:

APPETIZERS: _____

MAIN COURSE: _____

DESSERTS: _____

GUEST LIST

FIRST GUEST: _____

I have invited this guest because _____

_____

SECOND GUEST: _____

I have invited this guest because _____

_____

THIRD GUEST: _____

I have invited this guest because _____

_____

FOURTH GUEST: _____

I have invited this guest because _____

_____

Copyright © 1996 by John Wiley & Sons, Inc.

163. MAKING AND STAYING FRIENDS

Over a century and a half ago, Ralph Waldo Emerson, the great American essayist, wrote, "The only way to have a friend is to be one." In 1927, Elbert Hubbard in *The Note Book* wrote, "Your friend is the man who knows all about you, and still likes you." Like yourself, these two men thought much about friendship. Now you have your chance to write about friendship. In the spaces below, write ten rules for keeping a friendship strong. Discuss your thoughts with your classmates.

1. _____
2. _____
3. _____
4. _____
5. _____
6. _____
7. _____
8. _____
9. _____
10. _____

164. PARENTS

Here is your opportunity to think about those important people in your life, your parents. Like all other human beings, they have their strong points and their shortcomings. Though you might not always agree with them, they are looking out for your best interests. On a separate piece of paper, answer these questions concerning parents. Sometimes discussing the subject of parents with your friends can be quite helpful for all concerned. Try it!

1. I admire my parent(s) because . . . . _____
_____

2. If I wrote a thank-you note to my parents, I would thank them for . . . . _____
_____

3. Sometimes I have trouble talking to my parents about . . . . _____
_____

4. The activities that my parents and I share include . . . . _____
_____

5. An important lesson my parents have tried to teach me is . . . . _____
_____

6. I'm proud of my parents because . . . . _____
_____

7. An area of disagreement between my parents and me is . . . . _____
_____

8. My parents are proud of me because . . . . _____
_____

9. I'm sometimes embarrassed when either or both of my parents . . . . _____
_____

10. I'm like my mom or my dad in that . . . . _____
_____

11. My childhood is (like or different from) my parents' childhood in that . . . . _____
_____

12. If I become a parent, one thing I'd do that my parents have done with me is . . . . ___
_____

13. If I become a parent, one thing I would not do that my parents have done with me is . . . . _____
_____

14. A question that I'd like to ask my mom or dad but feel too shy or embarrassed to do so is . . . . _____

_____

15. My parents are different from most of my friends' parents in that my parents . . . ._

_____

165. THE SOUNDS AND MESSAGES OF MUSIC

Going back to the 1950s and the beginnings of rock and roll, and continuing on to today, music has always been an important part of the teen's life. Here are some questions dealing with music. Write your answers in the spaces provided and then discuss your responses with your classmates.

1. The purposes of music are to _____
   _____

2. A song that makes me feel happy is _____ because _____

3. A song that is rather depressing is _____ because _____
   _____

4. A song that has social significance is _____ because _____
   _____

5. A song primarily written for teenagers is _____ because _____
   _____

6. A song that I'd like to discuss in English or social studies class
   is _____ because _____
   _____

7. A song I wish I had written or sung is _____ because _____
   _____

8. A song that brings back a special memory is _____
   _____

9. A group or individual whose songs are full of meaning
   is _____. The main messages in the songs are _____
   _____

10. Music of today is different from the music of my parents' generation because _____
    _____

11. If your parents and you disagree about "your" music, how do you try to convince
    them that it is good music?_____
    _____

12. What song would be a good theme song for your class graduation or moving-up
    dance? Why? _____
    _____

Name _____ Date _____ Period _____

166. YOUR PERSONAL TIME LINE

In the spaces provided, list ten memorable personal events that have occurred in your life. You might include special occasions, significant achievements, important events, or anything else. After each event, tell why it was special to you. The events do not have to be listed in chronological order.

1. _____

   _____

2. _____

   _____

3. _____

   _____

4. _____

   _____

5. _____

   _____

6. _____

   _____

7. _____

   _____

8. _____

   _____

9. _____

   _____

10. _____

   _____

Name _____ Date _____ Period _____

167. A PAGE OF OPEN-ENDED QUESTIONS

Here is an opportunity to do some thinking about issues and feelings in your life. This page does not have to be shared with anyone else. It is strictly for your use. However, if you and your classmates would like to discuss some of these questions and answers, go ahead and do so.

1. Today I'd like to visit _____ because _____
   _____.

2. My favorite day of the week is _____ because _____
   _____.

3. I wish that my friends would _____ because _____
   _____.

4. My favorite aisle in the supermarket is the _____ because _____
   _____

5. If I could write a book about a topic I know much about, I'd write about _____
   _____.

6. A lesson I've learned in the past year is that _____
   _____.

7. A time in which I wish I had shown more guts was when _____
   _____.

8. In twenty years I will probably be _____
   _____.

9. My role model(s) in life is _____ because _____
   _____.

10. I'd like to change places with _____ for a while because _____
    _____.

11. I would tell the president of the United States that _____
    _____.

12. The problem I'd like to eliminate from the Earth is _____
    _____.

13. If I could relive a day in its entirety, I'd choose _____ because ___
    _____.

14. A word I'd use to describe myself is _____
    _____.

15. If I could be a character in a movie, I'd be _____ because _____
    _____.

168. WHERE YOU LIVE

Here are some questions dealing with the town, village, or city in which you live. Some of the questions might require a bit of research, but it will be interesting to see who and what made your place what it is today. The word "town" refers to either the town, village, or city.

1. For whom or what was your town named? _____

2. Approximately how many people live in your town? _____

3. How many schools are in the town? _____

4. Are there any colleges in your town? _____

5. What are some of the most common types of employment in this town? _____
   _____

6. If you were to make a video about the town, what five places would you definitely include? _____
   _____
   _____

7. What are some of the town's problems? _____
   _____
   _____

8. What is being done to solve some of those problems? _____
   _____
   _____

9. What are some of the changes that have happened within the town in the last twenty-five years? _____
   _____
   _____

10. What do you see as possible changes in the town during the next ten years? _____
   _____
   _____

169. A CHANGE IN YOUR LIFE

Life is never constant. When changes occur in our lives, we must adjust to these new opportunities and deal effectively with them. Sometimes we create our own changes, while at other times they are created by other people and circumstances.

Here are some changes that could occur in your life. On a separate page, write three effects that would be caused by the following changes.

1. Your dad or mom loses his or her job.

2. The school-year calendar now includes July.

3. Your best friend is moving away.

4. You win the million dollar lottery.

5. You take on a job that requires fifteen hours a week during the school year.

6. Your family moves to a new home seven hours away.

7. Your grandparents move in with your family.

8. You get the lead in the school play.

9. Your two best friends make the school team but you don't.

10. Your mom and dad are splitting up.

170. ARGUING YOUR CASE

Here are ten topics that could easily be argued intelligently from either side of the issue. Select one issue and choose at least four points that will support your side of the argument. Then select four points that your opponent could use against you. If there is time, select another of the ten issues and do the same.

Issue 1: In order to cut down on heating bills, the school calendar will be changed so that school will be open in July and August and closed during January and February.

Issue 2: The legal age to drive an automobile will be raised one year.

Issue 3: Videos that are in any way suggestive will be banned from television.

Issue 4: There will be no more assemblies because of the students' inappropriate behavior at assemblies.

Issue 5: The school day will be lengthened one hour for mandatory study-skills classes.

Issue 6: Those under sixteen must be accompanied by an adult in order to be admitted into the movies.

Issue 7: During their high school years, students must take a four-year sequence in each of the following subjects: math, science, English, social studies, and language.

Issue 8: Because of the parking shortage at the school, only ten students, selected by lottery, will be allowed to park their cars in the school parking lot. Since there is no other nearby parking facilities, all other students must take the bus or be dropped off.

Issue 9: Because of the budgetary restrictions, all students must pay a $150 activity fee per year in order to join athletics, music, or any other extracurricular activities at the school.

Issue 10: School coaches will be paid according to how well their teams do in the league standings. The higher the finish, the higher the pay.

ISSUE ____

YOUR FOUR POINTS: _____

_____

_____

_____

YOUR OPPONENT'S FOUR POINTS: _____

_____

_____

_____

171. LOOKING AHEAD

Let's look to the future. What's in store for you? Will you be a movie executive, a parent with four children, the next president? In the spaces provided, list ten personal events that you would like to have happen to you in the years ahead. Include possible marriage, children, employment, achievements, home location, and any other important aspects of your future. For some added fun, list the year in which each event will occur.

DATE   **EVENT**

1. _____   _____

2. _____   _____

3. _____   _____

4. _____   _____

5. _____   _____

6. _____   _____

7. _____   _____

8. _____   _____

9. _____   _____

10. _____   _____

Answer Key

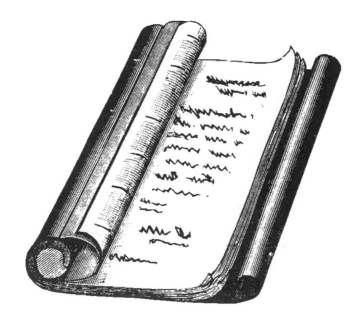

6. ACCIDENTS HAPPEN!

1. Saturday
2. spring
3. Neilson
4. Manning
5. Neilson
6. Manning
7. Neilson
8. restaurant
9. Fultoness
10. Masterson
11. third
12. 25
13. right-of-way
14. right
15. Masterson
16. Jackson
17. to take and hold in legal custody
18. scrape on the skin
19. Neilson
20. hit by Masterson's car which had been hit by Neilson's car

9. LISTENING WELL

1. Africa . . . 29 . . . grisly
2. Washington, D.C. . . . 9 . . . instigate
3. New York City . . . 100 . . . brand
4. Madrid . . . 50 . . . flaunt
5. Miami . . . 20 . . . abandon
6. South America . . . 52 . . . intimidate
7. Hawaii . . . 75 . . . harass
8. London . . . 1 . . . waver
9. Paris . . . 30 . . . allot
10. Los Angeles . . . 3 . . . shelter

19. THE WHO, THE WHAT, THE WHERE

1. p, q
2. g, r, a
3. o, t, f
4. h
5. j
6. i
7. u, k
8. s, m
9. d, n
10. c
11. b
12. e, l

20. PUTTING THE EVENTS OF THE TWENTIETH CENTURY TOGETHER

GROUP ONE	GROUP TWO
D . . . 1924	A . . . 1927
I . . . 1927	S . . . 1929
S . . . 1963	I . . . 1969
N . . . 1968	M . . . 1973
E . . . 1974	O . . . 1976
Y . . . 1979	V . . . 1982

The two famous people are *Walt Disney*, the creator of many cartoon characters, and *Isaac Asimov*, a prolific writer.

22. TIME MARCHES ON

The message is: FRIENDS HELP EACH OTHER.

F.	358 B.C.	H.	742	E.	1429	O.	1756
R.	800s B.C.	E.	986	A.	1508	T.	1770
I.	323 B.C.	L.	1096–1099	C.	1588	H.	1804
E.	44 B.C.	P.	1260–1294	H.	1620	E.	1861–1865
N.	30 A.D.					R.	1903
D.	425–450						
S.	632						

23. FRACTURED HEADLINES

A-I-Q-W	D-J-N-T
B-K-M-U	E-G-P-V
C-H-O-X	F-L-R-S

24. MORE FRACTURED HEADLINES

A-J-N-V	D-G-M-S
B-H-Q-W	E-K-P-X
C-L-O-T	F-I-R-U

26. THE WORDS (IN LETTERS) OF FAMOUS AMERICANS

1. Fourscore and seven years ago . . . (Abraham) Lincoln
2. Give me liberty or give me death. (Patrick) Henry

3. I have a dream! (Martin Luther) King

4. Ask not what your country can do for you: Ask what you can do for your country. (John F.) Kennedy

5. I cannot tell a lie. (George) Washington

6. Read my lips! No new taxes! (George) Bush

7. If you can't stand the heat, get out of the kitchen. (Harry) Truman

8. These are the times that try men's souls. (Thomas) Paine

9. You won't have Dick Nixon to kick around anymore. (Richard) Nixon

10. The buck stops here. (Harry) Truman

27. THE ABC'S OF GEOGRAPHY

1. Argentina
2. Brazil
3. Chile
4. Denmark
5. Ethiopia
6. Finland
7. Greece
8. Haiti
9. Iceland
10. Jordan
11. Kenya
12. Liechtenstein
13. Mexico
14. Norway
15. Oman
16. Peru
17. Qatar
18. Romania
19. Spain
20. Turkey
21. Uganda
22. Venezuela
23. Western Samoa
24. Yemen
25. Zaire

The unscrambled circled letters will spell Columbus and Magellan.

28. A STATELY FIND

A. Oregon
B. Kansas
C. Tennessee
D. New York
E. Maine
F. Wisconsin

29. COMPLETE THE COUNTRY

1. D   Australia
2. K   Belgium
3. C   Brazil
4. J   Canada
5. L   Denmark
6. A   Egypt
7. I   Greece
8. M   Israel
9. O   Mexico
10. B   Netherlands
11. G   Norway
12. E   Pakistan
13. N   Portugal
14. H   Switzerland
15. F   Venezuela

30. THERE'S ALWAYS A FIRST TIME

1. i	7. o	13. o	19. d
2. w	8. h	14. u	
3. a	9. o	15. r	
4. n	10. l	16. h	
5. t	11. d	17. a	
6. t	12. y	18. n	

The song is "I Want to Hold Your Hand" by the Beatles.

33. SPELLING TOWARD 67

1. commitment	9. villain	17. C
2. psychology	10. ecstasy	18. resistance
3. C	11. C	19. preferred
4. medieval	12. embarrass	20. separate
5. ninety	13. temperament	21. shepherd
6. cemetery	14. C	22. calendar
7. C	15. C	23. incidentally
8. government	16. boundary	24. violence
		25. absence

The numbers whose words are spelled correctly are 3, 7, 11, 14, 15, and 17. The total is 67.

34. CHOOSING THE CORRECT SPELLING

1. l	8. e	15. o	22. h
2. l	9. l	16. t	23. a
3. c	10. t	17. i	24. e
4. o	11. o	18. e	25. l
5. o	12. n	19. m	
6. l	13. h	20. i	
7. j	14. o	21. c	

The familiar names are all singers: *LL COOL J*, *Elton* (John), *Hootie* (Hootie and the Blowfish), and *Michael* (Jackson).

35. WHERE THE LETTERS BELONG

1. as<u>i</u>nine	9. ph<u>y</u>sique
2. critici<u>s</u>m	10. rep<u>e</u>tition
3. desir<u>a</u>ble	11. r<u>h</u>yme
4. fr<u>ei</u>ght	12. s<u>e</u>rgeant
5. hindr<u>a</u>nce	13. simil<u>a</u>r
6. inev<u>i</u>table	14. strat<u>eg</u>y
7. insur<u>a</u>nce	15. veng<u>ea</u>nce
8. li<u>e</u>utenant	

The six remaining letters are <u>e</u> <u>e</u> <u>e</u> <u>h</u> <u>t</u>.

The answer to a possible response to a joke is "TEE-HEE."

36. THE FORTY-FOUR HIDDEN NOUNS

 1. luck, instrument, foolishness
 2. Ellen, improvement, summer
 3. Wednesday, Howie, automobile
 4. toys, hugs
 5. athlete, pentathlon, Paul
 6. ecology, nature, students, world, humanity
 7. India, land, elephants, Yugoslavia
 8. officials, umbrella, assistants, rink
 9. education, medicine, asset
10. king, interest, newspapers
11. girls, opportunity, Thursday, hair
12. English, readings, Poe, Lawrence
13. answers
14. numbers, solutions

Lennon's quote is, "Life is what happens when you are making other plans."

37. THESE THREE LETTERS ADD UP!

1. GAB	11. EEL
2. MOB	12. BIN
3. RAW	13. YEN
4. FAD	14. CRY
5. DEN	15. PAD
6. ANT	16. NET
7. SIX	17. VET
8. DYE	18. VEX
9. LOB	19. NIP
10. SHY	20. ARC

38. VOCABULARY PUZZLER

1. O	6. O	11. S	16. S	21. S
2. O	7. O	12. O	17. O	22. O
3. O	8. O	13. O	18. O	23. O
4. O	9. S	14. O	19. O	24. S
5. S	10. S	15. O	20. O	25. S

39. ANOTHER VOCABULARY PUZZLER

Numbers 7, 8, 18, and 25 are synonyms. All others are antonyms.

40. MATCHING THEM UP

1. swagger
2. uproar
3. malice
4. spurious
5. stolid
6. reform
7. optimism
8. severe
9. inhibit
10. zany
11. submissive
12. ethical
13. enhance
14. durable
15. raucous
16. vague
17. stupor
18. antiquated
19. scale
20. trite

41. THE LETTER A

1. armor
2. axle
3. atmosphere
4. alibi
5. amen
6. adept
7. ado
8. allergy
9. advice
10. ace
11. abuse
12. abbot
13. acquire
14. Amazon
15. Aristotle
16. Arkansas
17. Armistice Day
18. Atlantis
19. Australia
20. Azores

44. LITERATURE AND AUTHORS (PART ONE)

MARK TWAIN

1. Missouri
2. Becky Thatcher
3. *Innocents Abroad*
4. New York
5. Halley's Comet

AMERICAN AUTHORS

1. Dr. Seuss
2. Edgar Allan Poe
3. John Steinbeck
4. Louisa May Alcott
5. John Updike

AMERICAN PLAYWRIGHTS

1. Neil Simon
2. Helen Keller
3. T. S. Eliot
4. Arthur Miller
5. *The Matchmaker*

45. LITERATURE AND AUTHORS (PART TWO)

AMERICAN POETS

1. Edgar Allan Poe
2. Robert Frost
3. Langston Hughes
4. Edgar Lee Masters
5. death

BLACK WRITERS

1. Alex Haley
2. James Baldwin
3. Toni Morrison
4. Ralph Ellison
5. Lorraine Hansberry

AMERICAN AUTHORS

1. F. Scott Fitzgerald
2. Emily Dickinson
3. William Faulkner
4. Ernest Hemingway
5. Gertrude Stein

47. SCIENTIFIC QUESTIONS

1. C
2. F
3. J
4. O
5. H
6. N
7. K
8. E
9. D
10. M
11. G
12. A
13. I
14. L
15. B

The three names are JOHN, ED, and GAIL.

48. WHICH SCIENCE????

The terms are primarily found in the following sciences:

1. C	9. P	17. C	25. C	33. C
2. P	10. C	18. ES	26. B	34. ES
3. B	11. B	19. P	27. ES	35. B
4. ES	12. ES	20. B	28. P	36. C
5. P	13. C	21. C	29. C	37. P
6. B	14. P	22. ES	30. P	38. B
7. P	15. ES	23. P	31. ES	39. ES
8. ES	16. C	24. B	32. B	40. P

49. THE TERMS OF SCIENCE

GROUP ONE	GROUP TWO
1. 3–C	8. 1–A
2. 4–D	9. 2–B
3. 1–A	10. 2–B
4. 1–A	11. 4–D
5. 2–B	12. 3–C
6. 2–B	13. 1–A
7. 3–C	14. 3–C

Each group has a total of 16.

50. FADED SCIENCE HEADLINES

1. Copernicus, sun
2. Harvey
3. Pascal
4. Isaac, Newton
5. Jenner, vaccination
6. McCormick, gin
7. Darwin, Species
8. Pasteur, germs
9. dynamite
10. Graham, Bell, telephone
11. Pavlov
12. Diesel
13. Marconi, telegraph
14. Einstein, relativity
15. Fermi, nuclear

51. SCIENTIFIC THINGS TO THINK ABOUT

1. No. Today we have a greater storehouse of knowledge to call upon and remember. Thus, it may appear that today's humans are smarter than their ancestors. But they're not.

2. The Colorado River and wind and frost are most responsible for the Grand Canyon being what it is today.

3. The horses use blinders so they would not become frightened or distracted by action happening around them.

4. The Tower of Pisa was built on soft ground and the foundation was not deep or broad enough to support the weight. As the Tower's center of gravity continues to slip away from the base, the problem of collapse seems more imminent.

5. A submarine has enough air within itself that it is lighter than water. Valves open or close to let water into or out of large tanks within the submarine. In this way the submarine can submerge or rise as need be.

6. Because men have thicker dermis, a layer of skin beneath the surface, than women do, they tend to have fewer wrinkles.

7. Red attracts attention more than other colors.

52. WHEN THE ACTION FITS THE MOOD

The words' meanings are as follows:

1. to show pleasure or joy
2. to show amusement
3. to charm or delight
4. to draw back in pain
5. to show either displeasure or concentration
6. to show amusement
7. to stare fiercely
8. to show malicious pleasure
9. to urge on
10. to express pain or disgust
11. to make a hoarse sound to show either great effort or annoyance
12. to laugh loudly
13. to wail or to laugh loudly
14. to show malicious triumph
15. to slander

53. MORE ACTIONS THAT FIT THE MOOD

The word's meanings are as follows:

1. to think about intently
2. to chatter
3. to cower; to draw back in fear
4. to tremble
5. to complain loudly
6. to show displeasure
7. to show contempt
8. to show either irritation or displeasure
9. to show either conceit or complacency
10. to show anger
11. to show scorn or contempt
12. to show worry or contempt

13. to repress
14. to show pain or embarrassment
15. to cry sharply

54. REARRANGING WORDS

1. laced
2. grown
3. saber
4. decorate
5. devil
6. carter
7. melon
8. brunt
9. north
10. clean
11. reward
12. sweat
13. charm
14. stink
15. strew
16. battle
17. sport
18. steal
19. shelf
20. madden
21. peach
22. trust
23. scalp
24. bleat
25. cheat

55. HOW A DEED BECOMES A STAR

1. bath . . . both . . . moth . . . mote . . . mole
2. save . . . sane . . . sand . . . band . . . bond
3. coat . . . moat . . . meat . . . melt . . . meld
4. flax . . . flay . . . fray . . . pray . . . prey
5. clay . . . cloy . . . clot . . . blot . . . boot
6. wind . . . wine . . . sine . . . sane . . . sage
7. fame . . . tame . . . time . . . tile . . . tilt
8. sure . . . sore . . . sort . . . fort . . . font
9. bank . . . bark . . . lark . . . lard . . . lord
10. grip . . . trip . . . trap . . . tram . . . team

56. WHAT IF THERE WERE NO VOWELS?

1. He who hesitates is lost.
2. These are the times that try men's souls.
3. Cleanliness is next to godliness.
4. A penny saved is a penny earned.
5. When the cat's away, the mice will play.
6. An apple a day keeps the doctor away.
7. The wisest men will follow their own directions.
8. Every cloud has a silver lining.
9. Conscience makes cowards of us all.
10. Knowledge is power.
11. Brevity is the soul of wit.
12. It is easy to despise what you cannot get.

57. THE DOUBLE LETTERS OF FOODS

beef   noodles
broccoli   pepperoni
butter   peppers
cabbage   pizza
carrots   pudding
cheese   rolls
eggs   snapper
herring   spaghetti
lettuce   stuffing
lollipops   strawberries
macaroons   taffy
mussels   toffee
                        waffles

Bonus Drinks: apple juice, beer, and coffee are possibilities.

58. LET'S ELIMINATE WAR AND HATE

COLUMN A   COLUMN B

 1. toward   1. heated
 2. wart   2. shatter
 3. reward   3. hearten
 4. swear   4. hesitate
 5. coward   5. chaste
 6. beware   6. exhausted
 7. wharf   7. phosphate
 8. homeward   8. whatever
 9. award   9. hearten
10. sweater   10. chatter
11. warrior   11. chapter
12. wearer   12. asphyxiate
13. inward   13. enchanted
14. swarm   14. annihilate
15. warden   15. hasten

59. THE ART OF DECODING

1.   Time is money.
2.   Look before you leap.
3.   . . . And I can't get up.
4.   Stand up and be counted.
5.   Good things come to those who wait.
6.   The proud, the few, the Marines.
7.   We pause for this commercial message.

60. HAVE A HEART

1. to be kind 2. to be watchful 3. easily accessible 4. not able to find the right words 5. one that brings on grief or sorrow 6. to know it completely 7. human cleaning effort 8. something that's not attractive 9. an attention-getter 10. to agree with 11. punishment equal to the one given out 12. to attract attention 13. to look at someone in an inviting way 14. to be out in the open 15. to look at in an amorous way 16. change of mind 17. to feel regretful or unhappy about something 18. to be well-meaning 19. to cause one to feel love 20. very sincerely

61. AN OUT OF BODY EXPERIENCE

1. ear
2. hand
3. head
4. mouth
5. foot
6. eye
7. lip
8. leg
9. heel
10. back
11. elbow
12. nose
13. neck
14. shoulder
15. tongue

62. TRIPLE PLAY

1. head
2. foot
3. set
4. king
5. sally
6. company
7. nerve
8. crash
9. quack
10. labor
11. corner
12. plate
13. paddle
14. cup
15. game
16. down
17. burn
18. last
19. skip
20. chuck

63. A TRIP TO THE RESTAURANT

1. beans
2. beer
3. carrots
4. chicken
5. clams
6. coffee
7. corn
8. cucumbers
9. lettuce
10. milk
11. potatoes
12. rice
13. shrimp
14. steak

64. A PAGE OF TOM SWIFTIES

1. m
2. j
3. i
4. c
5. b
6. e
7. n
8. h
9. l
10. k
11. g
12. d
13. a
14. o
15. f

65. ANOTHER PAGE OF TOM SWIFTIES

1. h
2. i
3. d
4. l
5. e

6. n
7. j
8. k
9. a
10. b

11. c
12. m
13. f
14. o
15. g

66. FIRST NAMES HIDDEN IN THE SENTENCES

1. Chad
2. Vince
3. Ellen
4. Steve
5. Irene
6. Kate
7. Ryan

8. Walter
9. Cheryl
10. Cathy
11. Amber
12. Karen
13. Fred
14. Denise
15. Gwen

67. COMPLETING THE PARAGRAPH USING STRONG VOCABULARY WORDS

1. tardy
2. wooden
3. tirade
4. sluggish
5. valid

6. diminish
7. surmised
8. pompous
9. rebuffed
10. sullen

68. COMPLETING SOME SENTENCES

1. ominous
2. synchronize
3. ratify
4. sporadic
5. monarch

6. stalemate
7. tranquil
8. vociferous
9. variable
10. kindled

69. RUNNING THE ALPHABET

Here are some suggested answers.

COLUMN A	COLUMN B	COLUMN C
a. argue	awful	astutely
b. break	boastful	bravely
c. concede	charitable	carefully
d. dread	doubtful	daintily
e. exert	excellent	elegantly

f.	foul	futile	freshly
g.	grow	ghastly	gladly
h.	help	healthful	horribly
i.	inquire	intelligent	incessantly
j.	joke	jovial	jokingly
k.	kick	kind	kingly
l.	learn	loving	laughingly
m.	merge	meddlesome	meticulously
n.	nudge	noisome	noisily
o.	operate	opulent	openly
p.	ponder	pretty	peevishly
q.	quiz	quiet	quickly
r.	raise	robust	rudely
s.	stay	stocky	strongly
t.	turn	tepid	truthfully
u.	urge	unkind	uproariously
v.	void	vile	very
w.	wander	wonderful	wolfishly
x.	x-ray	xerophilous	x-ratedly
y.	yearn	yearly	youthfully
z.	zip	zesty	zanily

70. MRS. MALAPROP HAS ARRIVED

1. sheep's
2. eggs
3. egg
4. drink
5. Curiosity
6. feather
7. chickens
8. place
9. eye
10. piper
11. thunder
12. red
13. horns
14. spill

71. READING IN A WHOLE NEW WAY

1. You are a cutie, Ellen.
2. You are easy to tease.
3. Are you okay?
4. You are excellent!
5. You are Katie's enemy.
6. Angie and Dee Dee are two beauties.
7. I'll double you.
8. Why are you being cagey?
9. Ann is sleepy.
10. The seas are empty.
11. Oh, why am I in ecstasy?
12. The tea and the wine are ours.
13. Are you forty-nine, Artie?

14. You aren't the one to see.
15. You are too busy to see him.
16. Bill is the foreigner.
17. One of you ate the pie.
18. I ate before you.
19. If the TV is okay, I am okay.
20. The candy is ours.

72. TED'S RIPPED SHOPPING LIST

1. apple	13. lettuce
2. asparagus	14. margarine
3. bacon	15. noodles
4. bagels	16. oranges
5. blueberries	17. peaches
6. broccoli	18. potatoes
7. butter	19. soups
8. carrots	20. spinach
9. candy	21. squash
10. chocolate	22. tomatoes
11. cookies	23. tortillas
12. eggplant	24. tuna
	25. watermelon

73. RECONSTRUCT A STORY CONTEST

The original sentences were as follows:

1. John's car broke down near Walnut Street yesterday.
2. The repairs were costly.
3. He needed a new battery and a new spark plug.
4. The mechanic fixed the automobile in less than an hour.
5. Today he will drive the car to Boston.

74. RECONSTRUCT ANOTHER STORY CONTEST

The original sentences were as follows:

1. I woke up late for school yesterday.
2. My principal punished me since this was my fifth lateness.
3. There were fourteen other students who also served detention.
4. Mr. Smith supervises the after-school detention.
5. From now on I'll listen to my alarm clock in the morning.

76. WORDS AND MESSAGES IN NUMBERS

1. A man, a plan, a canal—Panama

2. Step on no pets.
3. Able was I ere I saw Elba.
4. Sit on a potato pan, Otis.

Common trait: Each sentence is a palindrome which means it reads the same way backwards and forwards.

77. HALF A PROVERB HERE, HALF A PROVERB THERE

1. m	6. i	11. k	16. l
2. r	7. c	12. a	17. t
3. e	8. n	13. f	18. s
4. b	9. o	14. g	19. j
5. h	10. q	15. p	20. d

78. CHANGE THE FIRST LETTER AND CHANGE THE WORD

1. yellow, fellow, mellow
2. flatter, platter, clatter
3. willow, pillow, billow
4. light, fight, might
5. worry, sorry, lorry
6. sound, round, found
7. paint, saint, taint
8. cease, lease, tease
9. yeast, feast, beast
10. paring, caring, daring
11. brown, crown, drown
12. saddle, paddle, waddle
13. glower, flower, plower
14. mender, lender, bender
15. diner, miner, liner

79. LETTER PATTERNS

1. Starting with a word that begins with the letter *a*, each word starts with the next letter in the alphabet.
2. Every other word begins with a boy's name (Ken, John, al, tom, art).
3. Each word begins with two letters that are consecutive letters in the alphabet.
4. The twenty-four letters found in this sentence can be broken up into pairs of letters that are the two-letter postal abbreviations of the states. As an example, Many is Massachusetts and New York, and so forth.
5. Each word's first letter is also its last letter.
6. The last two letters of a word are reversed to start the next word.
7. The letters alternate with a consonant-vowel pattern throughout.

85. THE RIGHT WRITE THING TO TOO TWO DO DUE DEW

1. taught, taut
2. bored, board
3. vain, vane
4. fined, find
5. You, ewe, yew
6. toe, tow
7. great, grate
8. hail, hale
9. ate, eight
10. pain, pane
11. tale, tail
12. whether, weather
13. gait, gate
14. maid, made
15. groan, grown
16. sense, scents
17. pail, pale
18. wring, ring
19. wail, whale
20. break, brake

87. WHY IT HAS THE NAME IT DOES

1. It connects one side of the face with the other.
2. It is shaped like a bicycle's handlebar.
3. It looks as though such a person has just eaten something sour.
4. These whiskers, worn on the side of the face, are named after General Burnside who made them famous during the War between the States.
5. It is a rounded part of the foot.
6. It may have derived its name because the eye tooth has one long, straight root (like the letter *i*'s shape) or perhaps because it is located directly under the eye.
7. This probably has to do with Adam and the Garden of Eden apple. The Adam's Apple is primarily seen in men.
8. The legs are shaped like a bow.
9. The humerus is the bone extending from the shoulder to the elbow. Perhaps the pun is on the bone humerus (humorous).
10. One who is pigeon-toed has the toes or feet turned in, like a pigeon.
11. This finger is used most often to index things. It is a pointer or an indicator.
12. The patella or kneecap is exactly that, the cap of the knee.
13. Due to their late appearance in the mouth, supposedly when one has attained wisdom, this tooth is called the wisdom tooth.
14. Achilles, a Greek warrior and leader in the Trojan War, was killed by Paris with an arrow that hit Achilles in the tendon. Thus his tendon was his vulnerable spot.
15. Fallen arches look as though they have fallen from the foot.
16. The area above the eyes and the line where the hair normally begins is called the forehead. It's the front or "fore" of the head.
17. A crown is the highest area ("peak") of the head.
18. The belly is shaped like a pot if the person is pot-bellied.
19. The chest is shaped like a barrel when one is barrel-chested.
20. The forearm is the arm area between the wrist and the elbow, or the ("fore") front part of the arm.
21. The term comes from the jaw's resemblance to the early lantern with long sides of thin, concave horn.
22. A cherub is an angel who is chubby and rosy-faced. Thus the term cherubic face.

88. A SCORE OF ANALOGIES

The students will make up their own analogies, but these are the basic relationships of the words used in the exercise.

1. The duke is the male equivalent of the female duchess.
2. You investigate a crime.
3. A beret is worn on the head.
4. You dig with a shovel.
5. If something is ghastly, it will probably nauseate you.
6. A commander leads a company.
7. To mumble is to talk indistinctly.
8. A thermometer measures temperature.
9. The ceremony in which a priest becomes a priest is called "the ordination."
10. If you have more endurance, you outlast another.
11. They are opposite in size.
12. An aria is in the field of music or opera. Thus it is a musical piece.
13. A throttle allows one to gauge the flow.
14. A nutshell is a concise summary.
15. A ruffian is not a kind person.
16. They are opposites.
17. If something is vile, it is usually not attractive.
18. If a defendant is exonerated, he or she is freed from charges.
19. A misdemeanor is not as serious a crime as a felony.
20. A thief purloins or steals.

89. SEEMINGLY SENSELESS EQUATIONS THAT DO MAKE SENSE!

1. 365 1/4 days = 1 year
2. 2 feet + 12 inches = 1 yard
3. 11 months + 30 days = 1 year
4. 168 hours = 1 week
5. 1 day − 60 minutes = 23 hours
6. 100 = 60 + 40 (in roman numerals)
7. 52 weeks = 1 year
8. 1760 yards + 5280 feet = 2 miles
9. 720 seconds − 2 minutes = 1/6 of an hour
10. 25 hours − 60 minutes = 1 day

90. MYSTERIOUS SEQUENCES

1. Months of the year
2. Numbers
3. Colors of the spectrum
4. Planets in order away from the sun . . . Mercury, Venus, Earth, Mars, Jupiter, Saturn, Uranus, Neptune, Pluto

5. U.S. presidents . . . Washington, Adams, Jefferson, Madison, Monroe, Adams
6. Signs of the Zodiac . . . Aries, Taurus, Gemini, Cancer, Leo, Virgo, Libra, Scorpios, Sagittarius, Capricorn, Aquarius, Pisces
7. Units of linear measurement in increasing order . . . inch, foot, yard, mile
8. The first ten letters of the Greek alphabet . . . alpha, beta, gamma, delta, epsilon, zeta, eta, theta, iota, kappa
9. The notes on the lines of the G clef (in music) . . . every good boy does fine
10. The eight parts of speech . . . noun, pronoun, verb, adjective, adverb, preposition, conjunction, interjection

91. WRITING THE RIGHT WORDS

Answers will vary.

92. COUNT ME IN

1. odd numbers
2. months with 31 days
3. fast roads
4. Ivy League colleges
5. vegetables
6. board games
7. religions
8. palindromes
9. bones
10. explorers
11. parts of speech
12. African countries
13. baseball players
14. composers
15. ballet terms
16. women authors
17. wonders of the ancient world
18. letters of the Greek alphabet

93. THIS IS TO THIS

1. weight
2. man
3. teeth
4. visual
5. Massachusetts
6. green
7. racket
8. duchess
9. blue
10. machine
11. eating
12. elbow
13. musician
14. evict
15. China
16. play
17. finger
18. Deborah (Debra)
19. zip code
20. degrees

94. SERIOUS ABOUT SERIES

1	11	11.	70
2.	12	12.	3
3.	243	13.	20
4.	10.25	14.	29
5.	36	15.	1/128
6.	15	16.	45
7.	94	17.	8 1/5
8.	3.453125	18.	2.56
9.	684	19.	.64
10.	11	20.	344

96. THE SCRAMBLED-UP TRIOS

1. red, white, blue
2. win, place, show
3. readin, ritin, rithmetic
4. hook, line, sinker
5. lion, witch, wardrobe
6. vanilla, chocolate, strawberry
7. beg, borrow, steal
8. April, May, June
9. faith, hope, charity
10. past, present, future
11. tall, dark, handsome
12. liberty, equality, fraternity

97. MOMENTS IN TIME

1. No. Kennedy was assassinated in 1963 and Armstrong walked on the moon in 1969.
2. No. Presley died in 1977 and "Thriller" was popular in 1983–1984.
3. Yes. The Berlin Wall was demolished in 1989.
4. Yes. Washington lived from 1731–1799 and Napoleon lived from 1769–1840.
5. Yes. Baseball was organized when she was nine years old.
6. No. *Romeo and Juliet* was published in 1595 while Gutenberg died in 1468.
7. No. Columbus died 15 years before Magellan.
8. No. Pasteur devised the rabies immunization in 1885.
9. No. Monroe died in 1962.
10. Yes. Both lived during the twentieth century.
11. Yes. The book was written in 1908. Twain died two years later.
12. Yes. The swearing in was in 1981 and Gandhi died three years later.
13. Yes. CD's emerged in 1983 and Nixon died eleven years later.

98. IS IT POSSIBLE THAT. . .?

1. Yes. Ruth died in 1948, seven years after Gehrig died.
2. Yes. "Auld Lang Syne" was published in 1794 and Washington's presidential term ran from 1789–1797.
3. No. Dynamite was invented by Alfred Nobel in 1866, the year after the Civil War ended.

4. No. Tchaikovsky died in 1893 and the zeppelin was built five years later.
5. No. Ali retired in 1981. Tyson would have been fifteen years old in 1981.
6. Yes. Forks became popular in France in 1589. They could easily have reached London during the 1590s when Shakespeare was very popular.
7. Yes. Da Vinci died in 1519 and the pocket handkerchief had been popular for over a decade by that time.
8. Yes. Henry VIII died in 1547 almost a half century after black-lead pencils were first used in Europe.
9. Yes. Toll roads were introduced to England in 1269 and Polo died in 1324.
10. No. Robinson died in 1972, the year before the designated hitter was first allowed in baseball.

100. METS, JETS, NETS, AND OTHER SPORTS SETS

1. Montreal is a city in Canada.
2. Washington, D.C., is the capital of the United States.
3. The initial consonant sounds both have the *F* sound.
4. The Islanders play on Long Island in New York.
5. The maple leaf is a famous Canadian symbol.
6. Vancouver is in Canada and a "Canuck" is a French Canadian.
7. Oil is a natural resource found near Edmonton, Canada.
8. Ottawa is the capital of Canada, the home of the French government.
9. "Nordique" is French for a person from the north and Quebec is one of the northern cities in the National Hockey League.
10. Philadelphia, Pennsylvania, is the home of the Liberty Bell, the symbol of the Spirit of 1776, the American Revolution.
11. Boston is the home of many Irish and a "Celtic" is a descendant of a person who came from Ireland or close by.
12. Dallas is in Texas. "Maverick" is a word associated with a Texas farmer named Samuel Maverick who refused to brand his cattle. Thus, any cattle without a brand could easily have been the property of Samuel Maverick.
13. Indianapolis is the home of the famous Indianapolis Speedway. Thus a pace car or one who sets the speed is associated with this state.
14. At one time the Lakers were located in Minnesota, a state famous for its numerous lakes.
15. Orlando, Florida, is the home of Disney's The Magic Kingdom.
16. The New Jersey Nets were once located on Long Island where the Mets (baseball) and Jets (football) were also playing at the same time. The names seemed to go well together.
17. A Knickerbocker is a descendant of the early Dutch settlers of New York.

101. A PART IS MISSING

1. turn	6. double	11. red
2. hot	7. egg	12. square
3. last	8. field	13. white
4. gold	9. first	14. small
5. cherry	10. honor	15. yellow

102. KNOW US BY OUR SLOGANS

1.	c	11.	r
2.	s	12.	q
3.	b	13.	m
4.	h	14.	d
5.	j	15.	i
6.	e	16.	o
7.	n	17.	p
8.	a	18.	l
9.	g	19.	k
10.	t	20.	f

103. MIXED-UP ADVERTISEMENTS

1.	b	11.	i
2.	f	12.	r
3.	n	13.	c
4.	t	14.	h
5.	k	15.	l
6.	p	16.	m
7.	q	17.	g
8.	j	18.	o
9.	a	19.	e
10.	d	20.	s

104. DECODING THE MESSAGE

The concealed message is (f) WE NEED MORE MONEY.

105. THEY ALL ADD UP THE SAME

Though there are many ways, one way is:

4	9	2
3	5	7
8	1	6

106. NUMBER STUMPER

1.	17	4.	27
2.	83	5.	46
3.	38	6.	55
		7.	717

107. LARGEST TO SMALLEST

1. 1, 7/8, 3/7, .41, 1/16
2. 16/2, square root of 49, cube root of 125, 4/3, 9/14
3. 8/3, 1/3, 2/9, 1/6, 1/36
4. 3 squared, cube root of 343, 42/7, 25/5, 2 × 3/2
5. 55/3, 6 × the square root of 9, 101/5.64, 4.2 squared, the square root of 19
6. 71 divided by 3.64, 15.9 × 1.2, 16 divided by .98, 64 × .25, 19 divided by 1.2
7. 41 divided by 12.4, 29 divided by 9, 22 divided by 7, 25 divided by 8, 39 divided by 14
8. 7.4 × 7.6, 7.3 × 7.7, 7.2 × 7.8, 7.1 × 7.9, 7.9 × 6.6
9. 17 divided by 4, 21 divided by 5, 25 divided by 6, 29 divided by 7, 33 divided by 8
10. 41 divided by 14, 26 divided by 9, 23 divided by 8, 14 divided by 5, 8 divided by 3

108. SEQUENCING TO ONE

GROUP ONE		GROUP TWO		GROUP THREE	
A.	2	F.	5	K.	10
B.	9	G.	7	L.	6
C.	10	H.	8	M.	5
D.	6	I.	4	N.	4
E.	3	J.	1	O.	3

109. COUNTING YOUR CHANGE

	Q	D	N	P	
1.	0	0	5	0	
2.	0	0	7	0	(or 1 0 1 5)
3.	0	1	4	3	
4.	1	1	2	1	
5.	1	1	4	1	(or 2 5 1 1)
6.	0	1	1	2	
7.	1	1	1	3	
8.	0	2	1	4	
9.	1	2	1	4	
10.	1	2	2	2	
11.	1	1	2	3	
12.	0	2	2	4	
13.	1	2	2	4	
14.	1	2	2	0	
15.	3	1	0	3	
16.	2	2	1	0	
17.	1	2	0	2	
18.	0	3	1	1	
19.	1	0	1	2	
20.	1	1	1	2	

IIO. FIGURING OUT THE CHANGE

	GROUP 1	GROUP 2	GROUP 3	TOTAL
1.	2 coins	<u>3</u> coins	4 coins	9 coins
	11¢	16¢	<u>12¢</u>	39¢

The total number of dimes in the three groups is <u>2</u>.

	GROUP 1	GROUP 2	GROUP 3	TOTAL
2.	<u>3</u> coins	4 coins	5 coins	12 coins
	45¢	26¢	<u>18¢</u>	89¢

The total number of nickels in the three groups is <u>2</u>.

	GROUP 1	GROUP 2	GROUP 3	TOTAL
3.	7 coins	<u>5</u> coins	3 coins	15 coins
	<u>25¢</u>	31¢	35¢	91¢

The total number of quarters in the three groups is <u>1</u>.

	GROUP 1	GROUP 2	GROUP 3	TOTAL
4.	<u>4</u> coins	5 coins	5 coins	14 coins
	37¢	27¢	<u>46¢</u>	$ 1.10

The total number of pennies in the three groups is <u>5</u>.

	GROUP 1	GROUP 2	GROUP 3	TOTAL
5.	4 coins	<u>6</u> coins	4 coins	14 coins
	31¢	43¢	<u>41¢</u>	$1.15

The total number of quarters in the three groups is <u>2</u>.

	GROUP 1	GROUP 2	GROUP 3	TOTAL
6.	5 coins	5 coins	<u>6</u> coins	16 coins
	31¢	<u>18¢</u>	67¢	$1.16

The total number of dimes in the three groups is <u>4</u>.

III. THE BIG LEAGUES' SPRING TRAINING LEAGUE

1. California Angels
2. .313
3. 6
4. .016
5. .600
6. 4
7. Kansas City Royals
8. California Angels
9. Boston Red Sox
10. 4
11. 3
12. .833
13. Kansas City, .043
14. No
15. Yes

II2. THE PERCENTAGES ARE WITH YOU

1. 51%
2. 49%
3. 17%
4. 28%
5. 55%
6. 10%
7. 14%
8. 27%
9. 27%
10. 20%
11. 53%
12. 51%

113. THE CENTURY CLUB

GROUP ONE	GROUP TWO	GROUP THREE
1. 11	1. 21	1. 32
2. 32	2. 9	2. 35
3. 20	3. 24	3. 4
4. 9	4. 21	4. 6
5. 28	5. 25	5. 23

Common: ALL the groups add up to 100.

114. A TAXING SITUATION

1. $16.20	6. $6825
2. $58.85	7. set of posters
3. $34.98	8. $492.35
4. $24.30	9. $10,500
5. $20	10. $4,500

115. THE MISSING LINKS

(Read the numbers in each problem from left to right, top row first.)

1. 3	7. 9
2. 3	8. 8
3. 4, 1	9. 4, 2
4. 7, 5	10. 4, 3
5. 1	11. 0, 3; 1, 2; 2, 1
6. 4	12. 6, 9

116. A CAPITAL EXPERIENCE

1. A	7. D
2. U	8. O
3. S	9. V
4. T	10. E
5. I	11. R
6. N	

Both cities are state capitals. Austin is the capital of Texas and Dover is Delaware's capital.

117. MATH MATCH-UP

1. J	6. H	11. L	16. T
2. I	7. F	12. K	17. N
3. S	8. E	13. D	18. B
4. A	9. M	14. C	19. O
5. R	10. P	15. G	20. Q

118. ALIVE WITH FORTY-FIVE!

1. 5.4 miles
2. 8
3. $24,336
4. $120
5. $9870

6. $54,636
7. $43,200
8. 34 inches
9. $4.23
10. $2,100

119. THE ANSWER BOXES

1. 176 pounds
2. 6 minutes
3. 59 bottles
4. 270 CD's

5. 81%
6. $3,600
7. Fran
8. $14

120. IT'S STOPWATCH TIME!

1. 5 minutes
2. 21 seconds
3. 76 seconds
4. 221 seconds
5. 42 minutes

6. 5 1/3 hours
7. 9 1/3 hours
8. 60 minutes
9. 52 minutes
10. 1.5 minutes

121. MATH AND THE MOVIES

The three movies are, in order, *The Sound of Music*, *Lethal Weapon*, and *Rocky*.

122. THE PROBABILITY IS. . .

1. a
2. r
3. c
4. h
5. i

6. m
7. e
8. d
9. e
10. s

Archimedes . . . Greek mathematician and inventor of the third century B.C.

123. HARDER PROBABILITY

1. b
2. b
3. c
4. a
5. b

6. c
7. a
8. a
9. a
10. c

124. FIGURING OUT THE AGES AND NUMBERS

1. 4
2. 12
3. 30
4. 16

5. 6
6. 14
7. 12
8. 4

125. PENNIES FOR YOUR THOUGHTS

1. a   The pennies are 6,171 feet tall. The two buildings would only be about 45% of the pennies' height.

2. $12,250

3. a   The pennies weigh approximately 6,800 pounds. The 24 NBA players would weigh approximately 6,000 pounds using an average weight of 250 pounds per player (probably a bit high).

4. a   The pennies weigh approximately 6,800 pounds. If an average player on the high school team weighs 220 pounds (again a little high), the twenty-two high school players weigh 4,840 pounds.

5. a   14 miles
6. a   49,000 quarters
7. c   14 days
8. b   255
9. b   53%
10. 40%

129. HOW DOES IT MOVE?

1. flies
2. floats
3. floats
4. floats
5. rolls
6. rolls
7. floats
8. floats
9. flies
10. floats
11. floats
12. rolls
13. rolls
14. rolls
15. rolls
16. flies
17. rolls
18. flies

19. flies
20. floats or flies
21. rolls
22. flies
23. rolls
24. floats
25. floats or flies
26. rolls
27. floats
28. flies
29. rolls
30. rolls
31. flies
32. rolls
33. rolls
34. rolls
35. rolls

132. COUNTRIES, CAPITALS, AND CURRENCIES

COLUMN A	COLUMN B	COLUMN C
1. Australia	Canberra	dollar
2. Austria	Vienna	schilling
3. Brazil	Brasilia	cruzeiro
4. Canada	Ottawa	dollar
5. China	Beijing	yuan
6. France	Paris	franc
7. Germany	Berlin	mark
8. Greece	Athens	drachma
9. India	New Delhi	rupee
10. Ireland	Dublin	pound
11. Israel	Jerusalem	shekel
12. Italy	Rome	lira
13. Japan	Tokyo	yen
14. Mexico	Mexico City	peso
15. Norway	Oslo	krone
16. Poland	Warsaw	zloty
17. Spain	Madrid	peseta
18. Sweden	Stockholm	krona
19. Switzerland	Bern	franc
20. Turkey	Ankara	lira

139. MIXED-UP PROVERBS

1	is not gold.	7	before they hatch.
13	make light work.	4	there's a way.
3	perfect.	15	than never.
10	has a silver lining.	2	let live.
6	saves nine.	5	big oaks grow.
8	nothing gained.	12	is the best policy.
9	don't make a right.	11	out of mind.
		14	and eat it too.

143. MIXED-UP MOVIE TITLES

The titles in alphabetical order are: *Apollo 13—Back to the Future—Batman Forever—Beauty and the Beast—Beverly Hills Cop—The Bridges of Madison County—Dead Poets Society—The Empire Strikes Back—Forrest Gump—Free Willy—Honey I Shrunk the Kids—Indiana Jones—Jurassic Park—Lethal Weapon—The Lion King—Return of the Jedi—Star Trek—The Sound of Music—Star Wars—Who Framed Roger Rabbit—*

145. BUYING A CAR

Ad 1:   Ford 92 Crown Victoria, all power (steering, brakes, windows, etc.), low mileage, warranty, mint condition

Ad 2:   Mercury 93, 4 door, automatic (transmission), air conditioned, 32,000 miles
Ad 3:   Honda Prelude, automatic transmission, red, 5 speed, leather (seats), price is negotiable
Ad 4:   Plymouth 91, new tires, power steering, power brakes, air conditioned
Ad 5:   Camaro 89, automatic (transmission), low mileage, power windows, excellent condition
Ad 6:   Eagle 90, new transmission, 70,000 miles, white exterior, warranty
Ad 7:   Chevy 88, Beretta, excellent (condition) inside and outside, whitewall tires, asking $3,500
Ad 8:   Corvette 75, 4 speed (transmission), original owner, new engine, alarm (system), negotiable (price)
Ad 9:   Chevy Van 88, V8 (engine), new transmission, am/fm cassette player, loaded (with options)
Ad 10:   Buick 83 Regal, 8 cylinder (engine), needs brakes, dual exhaust (system), 77,000 miles

146. CONNIE'S CONFUSING CALENDAR

1. February
2. July
3. September
4. May
5. May
6. February
7. June
8. October
9. October
10. November
11. November
12. January
13. June
14. January
15. February
16. November

151. FINDING YOUR WAY AROUND THE LIBRARY

1. Philosophy
2. Pure Science
3. Language
4. History
5. The Arts
6. Literature
7. Technology
8. Technology
9. Technology
10. Social Sciences
11. Pure Science
12. Philosophy
13. Religion
14. History
15. Religion
16. Language
17. Religion
18. Social Sciences
19. The Arts
20. Literature

153. WHAT TIME IS IT?

1. D
2. I
3. S
4. N
5. E
6. Y
7. L
8. A
9. N
10. D
11. M
12. T
13. R
14. U
15. S
16. H
17. M
18. O
19. R
20. E

The two ten-letter vacation attractions are DISNEYLAND and MT. RUSHMORE.

Teacher Notes

Teacher Notes

Teacher Notes

Teacher Notes

Teacher Notes

Teacher Notes

Teacher Notes

Teacher Notes

Teacher Notes

Teacher Notes

Teacher Notes

Teacher Notes